The Russian revolution
soldiers and peasants' soviets
bourgeois state. Subsequent successful seizures of power in the
name of the workers have involved either peasant armies led by
working class political nuclei or, disastrously, the occupation of
countries by the forces of the Russian workers' state.

The bureaucratic leaders of European workers thwarted the
spread of the revolution. The isolated Stalinist bureaucracy
produced a consolatory myth: that Russia did not need such foreign
victories because it would achieve 'Socialism in one Country'.

To defy this myth, this book brings together documents by
Marx, Engels, Lenin and Trotsky illustrating the real history of the
strategy that won the Russian revolution and can win future working
class seizures of power. Inside, readers will find Marx and Engels'
"Address to the Communist League", Lenin's "April Theses" and
"The Tasks of the Proletariat in the Present Revolution", Trotsky's
"The Character of the Russian Revolution" and Mandel's "What is
Trotskyism?"

Resistance Classics

Building Unity Against Fascism: Classic Marxist Texts
Leon Trotsky, Daniel Guerin, Ted Grant

Foundations of Christianity: A study in Christian origins
Karl Kautsky, Michael Lowy, David Packer

October Readings
VI Lenin. Leon Trotsky, DR O'Connor Lysaght

The Permanent Revolution & Results and Prospects
Leon Trotsky, Michael Lowy

OCTOBER READINGS

The development of the concept of Permanent Revolution

About the Notebooks for Study and Research

The Notebooks for Study and Research are published by the International Institute for Research and Education. The Notebooks focus on themes of contemporary debate or historical or theoretical importance. Lectures and study materials given in sessions in our Institute, located in Amsterdam, Manila and Islamabad, are made available to the public in large part through the Notebooks.

Since 1986 we have published 50 issues in English. Since 1998 they have been published as a book series in collaboration with publishers in London. For many years we had a parallel series in French, the *Cahiers d'étude et de recherche* (currently under review). Different issues of the Notebooks have also appeared in languages besides English and French, including German, Dutch, Arabic, Spanish, Japanese, Korean, Portuguese, Turkish, Swedish Danish and Russian.

OCTOBER READINGS

The development of the concept of Permanent Revolution

Karl Marx, Frederick Engels, V.I. Lenin, Leon Trotsky and Ernest Mandel

Edited and Introduced by D.R. O'Connor Lysaght

International Institute for Research & Education, Amsterdam
Resistance Books, London

Both the International Institute for Research and Education and Resistance would be glad to have readers' opinions of this book, its design and translations, and any suggestions you may have for future publications or wider distribution.

Our books are available at special quantity discounts to educational and non-profit organizations, and to bookstores.

To contact us, please write to: Socialist Resistance, PO Box 62732 London SW2 9GQ, Britain, email contact@socialistresistance.org or visit: www.socialistresistance.org

Published by Resistance Books, October 2010
Printed in Britain by Lightning Source
ISBN 978-0-902869-81-3

Published as issue 50 of the *Notebooks for Study and Research*.
ISSN 0298-7902

Contents

OCTOBER READINGS

Introduction to the collected edition

'Why republish Marx? Why republish Engels? Lenin? Trotsky?'

This was the question posed at the beginning of the general introduction to these articles when they appeared as a series of individual reprints in 2008. By now objective conditions have changed radically. It is clear that capitalism has not overcome the cycle of boom and bust, refuting practically the chief argument used by that system's defenders against the many obvious arguments that could be used against it.

This change, and certain necessary corollaries, such as Marx' *Das Kapital* becoming once more a best seller in his native country, justify republishing these pamphlets in a single volume, to help the disillusioned and dissatisfied fight the system successfully. They justify, too, the new introduction for the single collected work.

There were three reasons for the decline of interest in Marxism from the eighties onwards. The first has been mentioned already. From the Second World War, the capitalist countries had organised their economies by using taxation to subsidise economic growth and avoid a new thirties depression. Voices in the wilderness denounced this policy as creeping socialism. More effectively, increasing numbers of entrepreneurs withdrew their capital from the developed states and provoked a new type of crisis in which the inflation produced by unplanned economic expansion combined with a decline in that expansion caused a situation combining stagnation and inflation: 'stagflation'. Unemployment and prices both increased. Socialists were too divided to use the resulting discontent to introduce socialist states as bases in a process leading to socialism itself; the majority were upholding the discredited capitalist policies. New capitalist governments revived the policies that had caused the depression.

It is a matter of history that the positive effect of this was minimal. In fact, the forms of Thatcherite and Reaganite economics were very different, the first being geared far more to budget balancing than the second. The result was that, aided by its commanding place in the world economy, the USA enjoyed a brief boom ended by a renewed crisis, whereas the UK did not enjoy any such thing; the government elected on the slogan that its predecessor was not producing work kept unemployment levels higher than that predecessor's over its sixteen years in office. Where Reaganites and Thatcherites both agreed was in that more should be given those that had at the expense of those who produced the wealth. Since the alternative was for the latter to seize state power and since such a seizure was equated even by most of the latter's leading spokespersons as producing inevitably an economy short on consumer goods and administered through a police state, the revived regressive economics were accepted until they led naturally to a new crisis. Reagan was prevented constitutionally from continuing in office but had his name jeered by audiences on American television. Thatcher's policy 'flagship', the regressive poll tax, had to be withdrawn and she was forced from power. What saved their overall policies was a new factor that disarmed their class opponents.

This was the implosion of the Soviet Union and the collapse of its former European satellite administrations. It got even greater significance by the tacit agreement between those regimes and their avowed opponents that they had 'actually achieved socialism'. They had not; their vulnerability to the world market blocked such achievement and the attempt to overcome this handicap by overwhelming repression was counterproductive in that it alienated from socialism altogether many particularly in the capitalist metropoles while acting as a break on the technological developments necessary to compete with capitalism. The result was a final failure that alienated even more.

The third cause for the disenchantment with Marxism is general disenchantment in future possibilities. Capitalism stimulated an assumption of progress, based on European (and, later, eastern Asian) peoples' improved living conditions that arise from the successful development of productive forces, particularly labour, but also natural resources. It is now being brought home that natural resources are finite and, worse, that their unlimited exploitation can threaten humanity. Said humanity has to make choices more consciously than before. This is not bad. Human ingenuity enabled these resources to be used productively and can be used to solve these problems by intelligent use of technical growth. The point is that such conscious collective decision making is beyond the scope of the invisible working of the market. Nonetheless, the overall dilemma's immediate psychological effect is to weaken faith in any possible major material and political improvement in life styles

So, even today, conventional wisdom is as opposed to Socialism, let alone Communism, as it has been since1800. For it, collective action is, if sustained, likely to lead to tyranny, capitalism is not perfect, but as near perfection as is possible in this imperfect world. With a minimum of regulation (more than before the slump hit, but still not too much) to prevent deterioration into monopoly, the law of supply and demand in the exchange of private property enables the individual, albeit, if fortunate, backed by a family, to decide his or her future, and contribute to the collective future through the market. This system has maintained the economic growth that will enable all to enjoy the lifestyle of the North Atlantic bourgeoisies in the best possible personal freedom. Inequalities remain, but become less important as prosperity spreads. Discontent with the ownership of large, particularly productive, property can be reduced by the spread of small private ownership.

Profits are, as stated by the capitalist, and capitalist ideologue, Ernest Benn, "1/ the earnings of management, 2/ the interest of capital and 3/ an insurance premium for the risk undertaken."[1] Marxism, who needs you?

The short answer is: the oppressed and exploited. Marxism is the developed weapon that they need if they are to end the overall division of society between haves and have-nots that has existed in various forms since private property began. Not all who stand with the underdogs are Marxists. Nonetheless, the possibility of their liberation can be fulfilled only through the Marxist strategy.

This involves understanding the world. Once this is done, it can be changed. Karl Marx did the first, but neither he nor his heirs were able to achieve more than a partial and impermanent transformation. Accordingly, it is well to clarify the human condition once again. Experienced readers can skip the next dozen pages.

The nature of Life is shaped by the material conditions in which it has to exist, and not by divine dispensation. This is a general rule; Marx' collaborator, Frederick Engels analysed it, and,

---

[1] Ernest Benn, The Confessions of a Capitalist. pp 97.

though science disproved some of his supporting examples, his overall argument holds firm.

Human life is necessarily different, because of its advanced nature. A human being can think, have ideas and express them, thereby influencing others and often, ultimately, society as a whole. This fact leads many to conclude that, as the gospel says, 'In the beginning was the word.' Yet it is safe to say that, at the end of the tangles of ideas and material forces, it is the latter that provide the initial stimuli for history.

Before history there were tribes of hunter-gatherers holding possessions in common. After centuries, groups of them in the Middle East found the river areas suitable places for practicing agriculture. On the evidence, they organised themselves as matriarchal societies still holding property in common. Such communal property relationships have lasted in humanity's overall life longer than private ownership. Nonetheless, such ownership was dawning. As population grew, different communities developed economically in different ways. Early agriculture could not supply resources for its areas, particularly when tribes that had not settled came looking for space. Communal clashes became wars in which the men, whose hunting role had been marginalised, found a revived importance hunting other people. They took captives whom they put to work as slaves. They had to protect their communities from their prisoners. A successful community found that it had to run two economies: the primitive collective and that based increasingly on slavery, and that its prosperity was based increasingly on the latter. The slave owners divided the slaves according to their skills. They formed states, governing as a ruling caste, able to relax their strictness by controlling the productive resources, particularly water. The slaves' own communities had been destroyed; instead they had to work for the ruling caste on an individual basis, the stronger ones exploiting the weaker. As population grew, so society's hierarchic nature intensified. Private property and economic inequality came together and were magnified by different conditions of existence.

These social structures spread across southern and eastern Asia and into Europe. Slave production enabled a form of commerce and towns to be developed. City states arose, usually to be conquered by the slave empires. There were two main exceptions to this. The Greek city states survived for centuries before succumbing and developed, while surviving, a body of political ideas that would inspire thinkers in very different environments. They were overcome by a militarised version of their kind from Italy, and became part of the Roman Empire.

This empire resembled those to its east, except in one basic fact. The older states, from Egypt to China were able to survive and renew themselves because they performed economic functions, mostly supplying water, that were too large to be executed on a more localised scale. Rome did not perform any such functions. Initially it built roads and founded towns, but it had no obvious function in maintaining the economic life of society. If anything, its attempts to do so were counterproductively heavy handed. It could not renew the fertility of the intensely farmed slave-run estates that came to dominate imperial agriculture. Essentially it was a true precursor of most future states: a military-political machine for territorial expansion and, increasingly, defence. When these functions failed under attack from foreign tribal groups its provinces were often happy to come to local settlements.

The result was that the fall of the Roman Empire in the west was not followed by any imperial revival. Instead, from its ashes came the beginnings of a new social order. The tribal conquerors were civilised enough to learn the art of slavery for themselves. In England it continued into the twelfth century. Nonetheless, despite the reduction in its population, the post-Roman states were too large to be enslaved for productivity. Slavery requires a certain minimum of order, economically as well as politically. The conquerors had to come to an arrangement with their new subjects to survive. It was easier for them to divide and sub-divide the new countries, tying the producers to the land rather than to individual slave owners, and to allow them a share of their product. The slave became a serf; Feudalism had begun.

The new order developed slowly with different results in different countries. It was least successful in those territories where the eastern Roman Empire had been most effective in its attempt in the century after the fall of Rome to revive its power in the west. In most of western and central Europe, Feudalism worked, the population grew again, slavery disappeared and commerce revived on the new basis.

With commerce came towns, but the merchants could not grow simply by maintaining slavery when it had practically vanished from the countryside, and when the feudal state powers were still too weak to be able to enslave their neighbours. It was simpler to recruit free labour to produce for them and to pay them a wage to keep them alive. Modern capitalism had begun.

This has been a success story far surpassing those of feudalism or slavery. It is the dominant economic system throughout the world as its predecessors were not. It has given the impetus to technological development that provides the possibility of a decent standard of living for all peoples. Its defenders claim that this would come about far more quickly were it not for individual greed reflected in state interference and organised labour practices in the metropolitan world and corruption in the semi-colonies.

It has major defects. Even before the current slump, within the imperialist metropoles the gap between rich and poor spread since the stagflation period. In Britain, 4,000,000 are working more than 48 hours a week, 700,000 more than in 1992. This inequality within the state is small compared to the inequality between Britain and other metropoles and the countries of the semi-colonial world. Nor are matters likely to get better. Here are some prophesies made at the height of the recent boom by Robert Shapiro, an American liberal Democrat, an acceptor of global capitalism, if less extreme than its neo-con defenders:-

'Europe's major economic powers ...will enter a period of decline characterised by socially scarring high unemployment rates and a politically "nasty" combination of slashed pension benefits and raised taxes..... Globalisation requires... bare-knuckled competition.....The unwinding of the welfare state promises of social democrats is comparable to the breakdown of the communism.....By 2020, there will be substantially fewer workers paying the taxes needed to support the pension income of a larger pool of pensioners. This leaves countries with both ageing societies and public pension systems with three options: raise taxes, cut benefits or increase retirement age.....Wherever globalisation and its technologies take hold, the return on investment raises and makes the rich richer while more intense domestic and international competition holds down most workers' wage gains even when their productivity increases.'

Nonetheless, Shapiro believes that capitalism: 'is not a matter of right or wrong, but 'simply the best way the world has at this time to generate growth and wealth.'

So, under this 'best way', the majority in the developed world can expect harder work for less with possible compensation in more and more consumer goods.

Matters may get better for the majority in eastern Asia and the semi-colonial world? Quite apart from the recession, even this is likely to be denied. As V. I. Lenin saw, the highest stage of capitalism is marked by a tendency to stagnate. This does not mean that new capitalist metropoles cannot develop. This is happening very obviously in China, India and Brazil. What it does mean is that it is more and more difficult for such new centres to challenge the old. Although these countries have abundant resources, it has taken them far longer to emerge than their predecessors. The capitalists of these latter have not helped. The semi-colonies' growth is slowed by global profits going to the metropoles often as interest on debt repayment. From 1980 to 2000, African countries repaid four times the total debt they owed the earlier year. The accusation that it is corruption that is holding them back ignores the fact that corruption in the semi-colonial world is as much a weapon of the globalisers as it is of the local elites, nor have the former any scruple about replacing the less corruptible with the more corrupt without consulting the majority of the population. In China, the multi-nationals encourage government suppression of the free trade union movement to keep down their labour costs.

In any case the petit bourgeois (let alone the bourgeois) north Atlantic lifestyle cannot be spread worldwide. Its existing level is threatened by lack of natural resources. Certainly, a private car in every garage for every family in the world is impossibility. The Green Parties recognise this, but their empirical approach to the problem, working within the commodity system, prevents their aims being achieved.

Capitalist apologists argue that private sector technology can resolve such problems. This ignores another aspect of the problem: that privatisation in education is destroying the environment necessary for investigation even into technical development. Reduced state resources and the corresponding increase in private funding make research centred on designated projects focussed on instant results. This factor was always part of the scene, but now it is dominant, as it has to be; the profit motive means speculating to make profits, not to find truths. Abstract speculation is diminishing and encouraged to diminish. Yet without it many intellectual tools necessary for new discoveries will not be developed. The failure to find new penicillin to deal with the superbugs is significant. Slowly but surely, the market is doing what state oppression did in Russia. These security pressures are reinforced by the needs of the growing struggle between the developed metropolitan states and the countries exploited by them.

On top of this, there is the consideration that much public service money is wasted on management consultants to see that what remains after their fee is spent wisely.

In another sphere, too, capitalism betrays the promises of its pioneers, as well as the assurances of its present day apologists. The readiness of capitalist corporations to corrupt governments and thwart democracy is notorious. The removal of capital from Britain between 1964 and 1979 was a major example, albeit an extension of acceptable capitalist practice. Even then there was a more brutal process masked partially by two facts. Most of it was accomplished in the semi-colonial world or in states where democracy could and often did work to rectify matters. Moreover, it was always possible to point at even more blatant examples of corruption and breaches of democracy in the self-styled socialist countries, in order to shrug off the suppression of democracy in Guatemala or Chile, for example, as necessary to prevent worse befalling or simply as an inevitable part of the *condition humaine*.

There are signs that this virus is infecting the countries that benefitted from it. Not one of these traditionally, Ireland is now at least a candidate member of their club, making it a bridge for company abuse to pass from colonies to metropoles. In May 2008, the Supreme Court declared the Chief Executive of the company DCC to have perpetrated 'a fraud on the market'. The company board rejected this finding and asserted its confidence in him, though, despite this, public opinion forced him to resign. DCC is internationally a relatively small player. It is only a matter of time before a multinational acts with impunity to defy the law of a major imperialist state.

This is not really surprising. The system is said to run on the enlightened self-interest of the individual, but who judges what is or is not enlightened? The market is the sole economic mechanism by which the sum of interests can be expressed and it cannot measure them. Only the state is allowed the right to dictate the limits of self-interest, and these are dictated as often as not by the self-interest of the capitalists themselves. Attempts by their employees to influence the system in their own self-interests tend to cause the bosses to follow their interests further by seeking centres of investment with less demanding workers. In the end, this is a form of the class war, the existence of which its practitioners deny, no less than strikes and lockouts.

In this environment, it is scarcely surprising that groups of the least enlightened potential entrepreneurs will decide that, after all, 'the law is a ass' and follow their perceived interests into the retailing of illegal drugs or the simple private enterprise unilateral redistribution of property. After all, the pioneering British capitalists initiated their economy in the midst of just such a crime wave.

More positively, capitalism's greatest achievement has been to supply the means for it to be superseded. Firstly, it created as its integral part a class of non-servile workers with an objective interest in replacing it by their own state power. Secondly, in, and out of their own struggles to overthrow the remnants of feudalism and establish their political authority, they created to guide that class to power important theoretical weapons. These were economics from Britain, the first state where the victorious capitalists were able to create a political culture in which they could concentrate on the art of maximising their profits, philosophy from Germany, where the capitalist class was too hobbled by local divisions and foreign invasions to put up a serious struggle for power, and politics from France, where the capitalist revolution went as far as it could. The combination is Marxism.

Its founders began it in their native Germany. Accordingly, they began with the philosophy, basing themselves on the teaching of the triple dialectic of G.W.F. Hegel but jettisoning his idealism while merging its concept of how it affected the universe with the basic facts of materialism.

The result came to be termed Dialectical Materialism, a term that can intimidate many aspiring Marxists. It is best understood in seeing it in practice, notably in history, as for example, inadequately, in the historical account above or in its highest forms in Marx' Eighteenth Brumaire of Louis Bonaparte, Engels' Peasant War in

Germany and (unfinished) The Role of Force In History and Trotsky's History of the Russian Revolution. Admittedly, beyond the basic materialism, the rules are particularly easy to over-simplify. Firstly, there is the dialectic itself, often summarised as a development from first cause (thesis), through its negation (antithesis) to the negation of that negation (synthesis). For example, capital expansion (thesis) develops into imperialist deceleration (antithesis), which contains, in turn, the conditions for a new form of society (synthesis) This is, however a formula; no more than in atomic theory can world history be reduced to such save in the most generalised sense. In practice, there is at any one time a whole series of dialectical processes interacting on each other to negate, to negate the negation or to start new processes. Similarly, to take the other popular formula, that enough of a quantity can change an item into quality; it should not be used to ignore the fact that the quantity or quantities have to be defined in each case. In fact, as long as the analysis recognises the material factor as first cause, all that the Marxist has to do to guide choice of action is to examine each problem in detailed context, socially and temporally. This may slow down performance of the revolutionary duty, but it will ensure that it will be done successfully.

The forms of the dialectic enable Marxism's critics to concentrate their attack on its materialism. Recently, Francis Fukuyama presented an historic overview centred on pre-Marxist Hegelian idealism, in which the idea of capitalist democracy became the ultimate synthesis, or absolute. Then the material facts of pan-Islamic insurgency and the metropolitan opposition to it negated his formulation. There are older, more basic and more lasting idealisms. All attack materialism as being the straightforward determinism of history by economic forces, which does not stop many of them trying to stop history be purely economic means as the Unionist parties tried to stop Irish nationalism at the end of the nineteenth century. It can be said, fundamentally, that there are three main idealist schools: the religious, the nationalist and the individualist (or 'the Great Men Theory of History'). The first is, of course, the oldest; its weaknesses are that it is inevitably subdivided according to religions which cannot themselves explain their different fortunes without resource to material intervention. The same applies even more to the nationalist school. As for the theory of 'Great Men', it would be wrong to deny the existence of the said monsters but rather to remark how often material circumstances thwart such greatness. Slavery removed the incentive for a classical Greek to invent the steam engine; the society had the technological potential. In the realm of war, too, history records many heroic and skilled commanders, from Hannibal to Yamashita whose victories could not compensate for their hobbling by their material context. Cutting across all these are the fatalistic traditions: regressive and progressive. The first (usually related to the religious approach) sees history as essentially degenerating from an initial golden age. The second (originally the British 'nationalist', or Whig) narrative sees the exact opposite. It is not possible to disprove either completely; the final triumph will be decided by human action. What can be said is that the first was the natural result of technological backwardness from slavery to early mercantile capitalism, whereas the second was as much the product of capitalism's ability to seize state power in the most populous country it had won up to then as was British political economy.

This leads to consideration of the economic details of Marxist theory. At its base is the question of value, of which the creation is necessary for any hope of human advancement. For the Marxist, as for the classical British economists, value is the result of human labour producing socially necessary goods. What complicates the picture is the private ownership of the means by which human labour produces them. With the state's support, the private owners claim the whole of this value less turnover and the cost of paying for labour. This payment takes the form of wages as under feudalism it was the balance of the landholding and under slavery it was direct upkeep. The product is the commodity. Under capitalism, the value-producer has greater freedom to move and can organise to force the work place owner to increase his wage. This can not be done indefinitely. The competition that exists between the privately-owned enterprises forces each to increase their profits to survive. On the one hand, this is done through increasing production until a better product or means of producing it drives it off the market or until the market is glutted. This contributes often to a crisis of over-production, such as the one from which the world is said to be emerging today. It means increasing the employees' exploitation through intensifying working conditions, as well as causing them eventually to lose their jobs and wages in many cases. The second means a more direct attack on the workers' living standards by trying to enforce cuts in wages and salaries. If the direct frontal assault fails, prices rise and inflation follows, but this does not benefit the property owner since because inflation increases non-labour costs, it reduces real profits more than wages. Increasingly, the bosses impose their own solutions to their common predicament. They come to depend on the banks, they seek to negate the effects of competition through combining in monopolies and, as can be seen today in the higher wage economies, they move their businesses abroad to where wages are cheaper. None of these is wholly satisfactory for them. The banks increase the pressure on the profit margin for their own benefit. Monopoly tends to breed inflation. Even exporting enterprises is a task often limited by the supply or otherwise of workers with the skills needed by the business concerned. Even so, commodity production is spread throughout the world and, with it, the crises that must accompany it. The economic power of the banks reached the point where, in the 1980s, Thatcher made the considered decision to abandon Britain's industries in their favour. Though the present crisis was created by their need to increase their profits, they have to be rewarded at the expense of the people at large. The alternative would be revolution, but this solution is still unacceptable because people believe that actual socialism has failed. As a result the uneven spread of world capitalism has nurtured rivalries between its older economies and its newer ones influencing the peoples of each to bond on cultural rather than class lines and handicap attempts to resolve the crisis scientifically.

The opponents of Marxism will oppose this analysis. Abandoning the theorists of capitalism to whom they pay lip service, they concentrate on the question posed by the fact that socially necessary goods have to be produced if value is to be realised: how is social necessity to be measured? Undoubtedly, the market, the law of supply and demand, is rather better at this task than the fiat of a bureaucratic state, however socialist it may claim to be. While the industrial expansion of Soviet Russia was unquestionably the economic success story of the first half of the last century, a large scale equivalent of the expansions of Europe and north America, it was accomplished with as much wastage human and non-human as those of its capitalist predecessors and in conditions that would handicap future development as those predecessors did not know.

For all that, this does not justify the idea that price is itself value ignoring the work supplying the commodity concerned.

In any case, the real price of many of the most basic goods is reasonably constant. The great Irish socialist play writer Bernard Shaw, who accepted the idea of the market as dictating value, believed that supplies of bread and milk could be efficiently nationalised. Of course there may be a shortage, but the price will increase with the labour needed to resolve it.

At the same time, the market is less efficient at evaluating certain basic needs. In the sectors where the state has provided services, particularly in health and transport, the market makes problems worse rather than better. In the increasingly privatised health services, bureaucracy is expanding at the expense of actual healthcare. The new roads have their movement curtailed by toll gates and are justified by cutting rail to the bone. In Britain, extending privatisation to the railways has meant larger rather than the expected smaller state subsidies, transferring taxpayers' money to the new owners. Improved services could be financed by increased taxes on the rich, though these would have to be reinforced by socialistic measures on a continental, and eventually a worldwide scale.

Fourthly, the market can be and is being manipulated. The inequality that is its necessary product distorts its workings to weigh its decisions in favour of the rich.

This is downplayed by capitalism's defenders, but, at the present time of general cuts in living standards, it becomes very obvious. More obviously, the capitalists' need for increased profits forces them to stimulate new needs for individual consumption. This use of advertising does not only boost profits but distracts people from questioning the system that needs them.

Such questioning faces a final answer; the only choice is one between the market and the command economy dictated by state fiat: either the unconscious merging of the wills of free people or the dictation of a small group, usually reduced in practice to that of a single individual. In principle, most people would choose the first. However, the choice is a false one. Technology means that the conscious will of each person is more easily assessed and related to that of others than it was in Russia after 1917. Education, the distribution of information, can help enlighten further the average will. (In Russia in 1910, the last estimate before 1917, only 21% of the population was literate7) As yet, these potentialities are harnessed for entertainment, though, in 1984, George Orwell prophesied that they might be abused. A truly socialist state could place them as means to develop a free popular consciousness.

That such possibilities exist justifies Marxism's third component: the politics of revolutionary France. This is the part without which the whole would be no more than an occult dogma. Its aim is to change the world. Its philosophy and economics are merely explanations necessary to this end.

That it is the French revolutionary tradition is essential. The capitalist state cannot be simply transformed into a launching pad for socialism. History has shown this, most notably in the course of the British Labour government of 1945-51, the most radical Labour government produced by that party. Despite being returned with a massive majority, and taking a number of measures essential to the socialist struggle, it lost its momentum within three years, in part due to its somewhat eclectic programme, but also because the state remained a capitalist one with the senior administrators having links with and career prospects in the private economic sector. Without a complete spring clean of the state power, such power will remain capitalist.

Happily, capitalism has itself produced the force that has to destroy it. In the working class, it has provided a force that has both the need and the work imposed discipline to do the job. This force exists in every country in the world, though in most if not all it will not be able to achieve its goal without acting as senior partner in an alliance with petit bourgeois forces, most effectively the peasantry.

Recognising this, the capitalists have developed many means of combating it up to and including physical force (another reason for revolutionary violence). However, their front line is recruited from the workers themselves in the leaderships of their own organisations. The fact that these officials have come to achieve for themselves better conditions than the workers they claim to lead gives them a major stimulus for conservatism and class collaboration. From the German trade union leaders barring the general strike strategy in 1905 to union participation in capitalist economic policy today, union leaderships have acted to dampen resistance to the said capitalist economics. This has produced an equally mistaken reaction: workers leaving the unions in large numbers.

The answer is political. The most conscious elements of the international working class must join a party to develop their skills and prepare the nationally-based risings that will make up the revolution to narrow the delayed reaction of the exploited and oppressed to slump that enables the propertied to benefit from the unemployment.

Such an organisation has to have a strategy reflected in its programme. It is to this end that this book has been produced. Because it was initially unprepared, the Russian revolution was in two parts, the first (February) establishing initial soviets of workers and soldiers along with a bourgeois provisional government maintaining the bulk of the imperial state apparatus, the second (October) led by the Bolsheviks, giving the soviets full state power and sweeping away that of the bourgeoisie. Of course, subsequent successful seizures of power in the name of the workers have involved either peasant armies led by working class political nuclei or, disastrously, the occupation of countries by the forces of the Russian workers' state. These, however, have been products of a theory that distorted the Russian experience

The old bureaucratic leaders of the workers of western and central Europe thwarted the spread of the revolution to their states. This left a new soviet bureaucracy, established in a country impoverished by war and civil war and learning quickly the vices of its formal opponents to the west. It used early ideas of the revolutionary leader Lenin to interpret Russia's own revolution as a necessary bourgeois power seizure that would be the template for future successes. When these failed, they produced a consolatory myth: that Russia did not need such foreign victories because it would achieve 'Socialism in one Country'. Save under exceptional leaders, as in China and Vietnam, the other Communist Parties began to see their main tasks as defending Russia. The Russians themselves could defend their economy against the world commodity market only by draconian measures that failed at last.

For this reason, this book presents documents illustrating the history of the strategy that won the Russian revolution and can win future working class seizures of power.

D. R. O'Connor Lysaght.
2010.

23

Introduction to "To the Communist League"

The Addresses to the Communist League were drafted in March and June 1850. Two years and four months before, Engels had published Principles of Communism1. Four months after that, Marx and he had published the Manifesto of the Communist Party and its locally more specific 'Demands of the Communist Party in Germany'. Since then, Europe had moved from a revolutionary situation to the aftermath of successful counter-revolution.

Accordingly, unlike the early works mentioned, the Appeals were drafted for the internal membership of the Communist League, handwritten and passed around in manuscript. Not until 1885, did Engels publish them in full and then as an appendix to Marx' republished pamphlet on the 1852 trial of their Communist comrades. By then, their significance seemed only historical. Mass parties were paying lip service to Marx and Engels; they would found a new international in 1889.

Today, with the mass socialist parties surrendering to capital, the Addresses have a new relevance. They present a strategy for socialists to plan for the working class seizure of state power in a non-immediately revolutionary situation (although their authors maintained that a new revolution was closer than it was). While openly bourgeois parties claimed to head the cause of democracy, the Communists were warned not to liquidate their small organisation into these bodies, bur rather to work to take up their most militant demands, to set the pace of the struggle as the best builders for the future Communist order. If the Democrats took state power, they should oppose them eventually in arms. They should call particularly for a democratic constituent assembly, a centralised government and collectivisation of land. However, the second of these was modified by Engels in 1885. The last had to be abandoned by the Bolsheviks to win the peasant majority of Russians.) These demands were international in scope as was shown by the authors' combining emphasis on Germany with the perspective of immediate revolution in France and, in the second address, by their examination of the League as an international body.

It should be added that their call for 'the revolution in permanence' inspired Leon Trotsky's idea of the strategy that won temporary state power for the Russian workers. In 1924, his opponent, Josef Stalin tried to turn it against him by quoting from the First Address out of context. In fact, the Addresses contradict Stalin's actual strategies, third period, Popular Frontism and Socialism in one Country.

Hopefully this republication will help make this clear.

Marx & Engels: Address of the Central Committee to the Communist League

In the two revolutionary years of 1848-49 the League proved itself in two ways. First, its members everywhere involved themselves energetically in the movement and stood in the front ranks of the only decisively revolutionary class, the proletariat, in the press, on the barricades and on the battlefields. The League further proved itself in that its understanding of the movement, as expressed in the circulars issued by the Congresses and the Central Committee of 1847 and in the Manifesto of the Communist Party, has been shown to be the only correct one, and the expectations expressed in these documents have been completely fulfilled. This previously only propagated by the League in secret, is now on everyone's lips and is preached openly in the market place. At the same time, however, the formerly strong organization of the League has been considerably weakened. A large number of members who were directly involved in the movement thought that the time for secret societies was over and that public action alone was sufficient. The individual districts and communes allowed their connections with the Central Committee to weaken and gradually become dormant. So, while the democratic party, the party of the petty bourgeoisie, has become more and more organized in Germany, the workers' party has lost its only firm foothold, remaining organized at best in individual localities for local purposes; within the general movement it has consequently come under the complete domination and leadership of the petty-bourgeois democrats. This situation cannot be allowed to continue; the independence of the workers must be restored. The Central Committee recognized this necessity and it therefore sent an emissary, Joseph Moll, to Germany in the winter of 1848-9 to reorganize the League. Moll's mission, however, failed to produce any lasting effect, partly because the German workers at that time had not enough experience and partly because it was interrupted by the insurrection last May. Moll himself took up arms, joined the Baden-Palatinate army and fell on 29 June in the battle of the River Murg. The League lost in him one of the oldest, most active and most reliable members, who had been involved in all the Congresses and Central Committees and had earlier conducted a series of missions with great success. Since the defeat of the German and French revolutionary parties in July 1849, almost all the members of the Central Committee have reassembled in London: they have replenished their numbers with new revolutionary forces and set about reorganizing the League with renewed zeal.

This reorganization can only be achieved by an emissary, and the Central Committee considers it most important to dispatch the emissary at this very moment, when a new revolution is imminent, that is, when the workers' party must go into battle with the maximum degree of organization, unity and independence, so that it is not exploited and taken in tow by the bourgeoisie as in 1848.

We told you already in 1848, brothers, that the German liberal bourgeoisie would soon come to power and would immediately turn its newly won power against the workers. You have seen how this forecast came true. It was indeed the bourgeoisie which took possession of the state authority in the wake of the March movement of 1848 and used this power to drive the workers, its allies in the struggle, back into their former oppressed position. Although the bourgeoisie could accomplish this only by entering into an alliance with the feudal party, which had been defeated in March, and eventually even had to surrender power once more to this feudal absolutist party, it has nevertheless secured favourable conditions for itself. In view of the government's financial difficulties, these conditions would ensure that power would in the long run fall into its hands again and that all its interests would be secured, if it were possible for the revolutionary movement to assume from now on a so-called peaceful course of development. In order to guarantee its power the bourgeoisie would not even need to arouse hatred by taking violent measures against the people, as all of these violent measures have already been carried out by the feudal counter-revolution. But events will not take this peaceful course. On the contrary, the revolution which will accelerate the course of events is imminent, whether it is initiated by an independent rising of the French proletariat or by an invasion of the revolutionary Babel by the Holy Alliance.

The treacherous role that the German liberal bourgeoisie played against the people in 1848 will be assumed in the coming revolution by the democratic petty bourgeoisie, which now occupies the same position in the opposition as the liberal bourgeoisie did before 1848. This democratic party, which is far more dangerous for the workers than were the liberals earlier, is composed of three elements: 1) the most progressive elements of the big bourgeoisie, who pursue the goal of the immediate and complete overthrow of feudalism and absolutism. This fraction is represented by the former Berlin Vereinbarer, the tax resisters; 2) The constitutional-democratic petty bourgeois, whose main aim during the previous movement was the formation of a more or less democratic federal state; this is what their representative, the Left in the Frankfurt Assembly and later the Stuttgart parliament, worked for, as they themselves did in the Reich Constitution Campaign; 3) The republican petty bourgeois, whose ideal is a German federal republic similar to that in Switzerland and who now call themselves 'red' and 'social-democratic' because they cherish the pious wish to abolish the pressure exerted by big capital on small capital, by the big bourgeoisie on the petty bourgeoisie. The representatives of this fraction were the members of the democratic congresses and committees, the leaders of the democratic associations and the editors of the democratic newspapers.

After their defeat all these fractions claim to be 'republicans' or 'reds', just as at the present time members of the republican petty bourgeoisie in France call themselves 'socialists'. Where, as in Wurtemberg, Bavaria, etc., they still find a chance to pursue their ends by constitutional means, they seize the opportunity to retain their old phrases and prove by their actions that they have not changed in the least. Furthermore, it goes without saying that the changed name of this party does not alter in the least its relationship to the workers but merely proves that it is now obliged to form a front against the bourgeoisie, which has united with absolutism, and to seek the support of the proletariat.

The petty-bourgeois democratic party in Germany is very powerful. It not only embraces the great majority of the urban middle class, the small industrial merchants and master craftsmen; it also includes among its followers the peasants and rural proletariat in so far as the latter has not yet found support among the independent proletariat of the towns.

The relationship of the revolutionary workers' party to the petty-bourgeois democrats is this: it cooperates with them against the party which they aim to overthrow; it opposes them wherever they wish to secure their own position.

The democratic petty bourgeois, far from wanting to transform the whole society in the interests of the revolutionary proletarians, only aspire to a change in social conditions which will make the existing society as tolerable and comfortable for themselves as possible. They therefore demand above all else a reduction in government spending through a restriction of the bureaucracy and the transference of the major tax burden into the large landowners and bourgeoisie. They further demand the removal of the pressure exerted by big capital on small capital through the establishment of public credit institutions and the passing of laws against usury, whereby it would be possible for themselves and the peasants to receive advances on favourable terms from the state instead of from capitalists; also, the introduction of bourgeois property relationships on land through the complete abolition of feudalism. In order to achieve all this they require a democratic form of government, either constitutional or republican, which would give them and their peasant allies the majority; they also require a democratic system of local government to give them direct control over municipal property and over a series of political offices at present in the hands of the bureaucrats.

The rule of capital and its rapid accumulation is to be further counteracted, partly by a curtailment of the right of inheritance, and partly by the transference of as much employment as possible to the state. As far as the workers are concerned one thing, above all, is definite: they are to remain wage labourers as before. However, the democratic petty bourgeois want better wages and security for the workers, and hope to achieve this by an extension of state employment and by welfare measures; in short, they hope to bribe the workers with a more or less disguised form of alms and to break their revolutionary strength by temporarily rendering their situation tolerable. The demands of petty-bourgeois democracy summarized here are not expressed by all sections of it at once, and in their totality they are the explicit goal of only a very few of its followers. The further particular individuals or fractions of the petty bourgeoisie advance, the more of these demands they will explicitly adopt, and the few who recognize their own programme in what has been mentioned above might well believe they have put forward the maximum that can be demanded from the revolution. But these demands can in no way satisfy the party of the proletariat. While the democratic petty bourgeois want to bring the revolution to an end as quickly as possible, achieving at most the aims already mentioned, it is our interest and our task to make the revolution permanent until all the more or less propertied classes have been driven from their ruling positions, until the proletariat has conquered state power and until the association of the proletarians has progressed sufficiently far – not only in one country but in all the leading countries of the world – that competition between the proletarians of these countries ceases and at least the decisive forces of production are concentrated in the hands of the workers. Our concern cannot simply be to modify private property, but to abolish it, not to hush up class antagonisms but to abolish classes, not to improve the existing society but to found a new one. There is no doubt that during the further course of the revolution in Germany, the petty-bourgeois democrats will for the moment acquire a predominant influence. The question is, therefore, what is to be the attitude of the proletariat, and in particular of the League towards them:

1) While present conditions continue, in which the petty-bourgeois democrats are also oppressed;

2) In the coming revolutionary struggle, which will put them in a dominant position;

3) After this struggle, during the period of petty-bourgeois predominance over the classes which have been overthrown and over the proletariat.

1. At the moment, while the democratic petty bourgeois are everywhere oppressed, they preach to the proletariat general unity and reconciliation; they extend the hand of friendship, and seek to found a great opposition party which will embrace all shades of democratic opinion; that is, they seek to ensnare the workers in a party organization in which general social-democratic phrases prevail while their particular interests are kept hidden behind, and in which, for the sake of preserving the peace, the specific demands of the proletariat may not be presented. Such a unity would be to their advantage alone and to the complete disadvantage of the proletariat. The proletariat would lose all its hard-won independent position and be reduced once more to a mere appendage of official bourgeois democracy. This unity must therefore be resisted in the most decisive manner. Instead of lowering themselves to the level of an applauding chorus, the workers, and above all the League, must work for the creation of an independent organization of the workers' party, both secret and open, and alongside the official democrats, and the League must aim to make every one of its communes a centre and nucleus of workers' associations in which the position and interests of the proletariat can be discussed free from bourgeois influence. How serious the bourgeois democrats are about an alliance in which the proletariat has equal power and equal rights is demonstrated by the Breslau democrats, who are conducting a furious campaign in their organ, the *Neue Oder Zeitung*, against independently organized workers, whom they call 'socialists'. In the event of a struggle against a common enemy a special alliance is unnecessary. As soon as such an enemy has to be fought directly, the interests of both parties will coincide for the moment and an association of momentary expedience will arise spontaneously in the future, as it has in the past. It goes without saying that in the bloody conflicts to come, as in all others, it will be the workers, with their courage, resolution and self-sacrifice, who will be chiefly responsible

for achieving victory. As in the past, so in the coming struggle also, the petty bourgeoisie, to a man, will hesitate as long as possible and remain fearful, irresolute and inactive; but when victory is certain it will claim it for itself and will call upon the workers to behave in an orderly fashion, to return to work and to prevent so-called excesses, and it will exclude the proletariat from the fruits of victory. It does not lie within the power of the workers to prevent the petty-bourgeois democrats from doing this; but it does lie within their power to make it as difficult as possible for the petty bourgeoisie to use its power against the armed proletariat, and to dictate such conditions to them that the rule of the bourgeois democrats, from the very first, will carry within it the seeds of its own destruction, and its subsequent displacement by the proletariat will be made considerably easier. Above all, during and immediately after the struggle the workers, as far as it is at all possible, must oppose bourgeois attempts at pacification and force the democrats to carry out their terroristic phrases. They must work to ensure that the immediate revolutionary excitement is not suddenly suppressed after the victory. On the contrary, it must be sustained as long as possible. Far from opposing the so-called excesses – instances of popular vengeance against hated individuals or against public buildings with which hateful memories are associated – the workers' party must not only tolerate these actions but must even give them direction. During and after the struggle the workers must at every opportunity put forward their own demands against those of the bourgeois democrats. They must demand guarantees for the workers as soon as the democratic bourgeoisie sets about taking over the government. They must achieve these guarantees by force if necessary, and generally make sure that the new rulers commit themselves to all possible concessions and promises – the surest means of compromising them. They must check in every way and as far as is possible the victory euphoria and enthusiasm for the new situation which follow every successful street battle, with a cool and cold-blooded analysis of the situation and with undisguised mistrust of the new government. Alongside the new official governments they must simultaneously establish their own revolutionary workers' governments, either in the form of local executive committees and councils or through workers' clubs or committees, so that the bourgeois-democratic governments not only immediately lost the support of the workers but find themselves from the very beginning supervised and threatened by authorities behind which stand the whole mass of the workers. In a word, from the very moment of victory the workers' suspicion must be directed no longer against the defeated reactionary party but against their former ally, against the party which intends to exploit the common victory for itself.

2. To be able forcefully and threateningly to oppose this party, whose betrayal of the workers will begin with the very first hour of victory, the workers must be armed and organized. The whole proletariat must be armed at once with muskets, rifles, cannon and ammunition, and the revival of the old-style citizens' militia, directed against the workers, must be opposed. Where the formation of this militia cannot be prevented, the workers must try to organize themselves independently as a proletarian guard, with elected leaders and with their own elected general staff; they must try to place themselves not under the orders of the state authority but of the revolutionary local councils set up by the workers. Where the workers are employed by the state, they must arm and organize themselves into special corps with elected leaders, or as a part of the proletarian guard. Under no pretext should arms and ammunition be surrendered; any attempt to disarm the workers must be frustrated, by force if necessary. The destruction of the bourgeois democrats' influence over the workers, and the enforcement of conditions which will compromise the rule of bourgeois democracy, which is for the moment inevitable, and make it as difficult as possible – these are the main points which the proletariat and therefore the League must keep in mind during and after the approaching uprising.

3. As soon as the new governments have established themselves, their struggle against the workers will begin. If the workers are to be able to forcibly oppose the democratic petty bourgeois it is essential above all for them to be independently organized and centralized in clubs. At the soonest possible moment after the overthrow of the present governments, the Central Committee will come to Germany and will immediately convene a Congress, submitting to it the necessary proposals for the centralization of the workers' clubs under a directorate established at the movement's centre of operations. The speedy organization of at least provincial connections between the workers' clubs is one of the prime requirements for the strengthening and development of the workers' party; the immediate result of the overthrow of the existing governments will be the election of a national representative body. Here the proletariat must take care: 1) that by sharp practices local authorities and government commissioners do not, under any pretext whatsoever, exclude any section of workers; 2)

that workers' candidates are nominated everywhere in opposition to bourgeois-democratic candidates. As far as possible they should be League members and their election should be pursued by all possible means. Even where there is no prospect of achieving their election the workers must put up their own candidates to preserve their independence, to gauge their own strength and to bring their revolutionary position and party standpoint to public attention. They must not be led astray by the empty phrases of the democrats, who will maintain that the workers' candidates will split the democratic party and offer the forces of reaction the chance of victory. All such talk means, in the final analysis, that the proletariat is to be swindled. The progress which the proletarian party will make by operating independently in this way is infinitely more important than the disadvantages resulting from the presence of a few reactionaries in the representative body. If the forces of democracy take decisive, terroristic action against the reaction from the very beginning, the reactionary influence in the election will already have been destroyed.

The first point over which the bourgeois democrats will come into conflict with the workers will be the abolition of feudalism as in the first French revolution, the petty bourgeoisie will want to give the feudal lands to the peasants as free property; that is, they will try to perpetrate the existence of the rural proletariat, and to form a petty-bourgeois peasant class which will be subject to the same cycle of impoverishment and debt which still afflicts the French peasant. The workers must oppose this plan both in the interest of the rural proletariat and in their own interest. They must demand that the confiscated feudal property remain state property and be used for workers' colonies, cultivated collectively by the rural proletariat with all the advantages of large-scale farming and where the principle of common property will immediately achieve a sound basis in the midst of the shaky system of bourgeois property relations. Just as the democrats ally themselves with the peasants, the workers must ally themselves with the rural proletariat.

The democrats will either work directly towards a federated republic, or at least, if they cannot avoid the one and indivisible republic they will attempt to paralyze the central government by granting the municipalities and provinces the greatest possible autonomy and independence. In opposition to this plan the workers must not only strive for one and indivisible German republic, but also, within this republic, for the most decisive centralization of power in the hands of the state authority. They should not let themselves be led astray by empty democratic talk about the freedom of the municipalities, self-government, etc. In a country like Germany, where so many remnants of the Middle Ages are still to be abolished, where so much local and provincial obstinacy has to be broken down, it cannot under any circumstances be tolerated that each village, each town and each province may put up new obstacles in the way of revolutionary activity, which can only be developed with full efficiency from a central point. A renewal of the present situation, in which the Germans have to wage a separate struggle in each town and province for the same degree of progress, can also not be tolerated. Least of all can a so-called free system of local government be allowed to perpetuate a form of property which is more backward than modern private property and which is everywhere and inevitably being transformed into private property; namely communal property, with its consequent disputes between poor and rich communities. Nor can this so-called free system of local government be allowed to perpetuate, side by side with the state civil law, the existence of communal civil law with its sharp practices directed against the workers. As in France in 1793, it is the task of the genuinely revolutionary party in Germany to carry through the strictest centralization. [It must be recalled today that this passage is based on a misunderstanding. At that time – thanks to the Bonapartist and liberal falsifiers of history – it was considered as established that the French centralised machine of administration had been introduced by the Great Revolution and in particular that it had been used by the Convention as an indispensable and decisive weapon for defeating the royalist and federalist reaction and the external enemy. It is now, however, a well-known fact that throughout the revolution, up to the eighteenth Brumaire, the whole administration of the *départements, arrondissements* and *communes* consisted of authorities elected by, the respective constituents themselves, and that these authorities acted with complete freedom within the general state laws; that precisely this provincial and local self-government, similar to the American, became the most powerful lever of the revolution and indeed to such an extent that Napoleon, immediately after his coup d'état of the eighteenth Brumaire, hastened to replace it by the still existing administration by prefects, which, therefore, was a pure instrument of reaction from the beginning. But no more than local and provincial self-government is in contradiction to political, national centralisation, is it necessarily bound up with that narrow-minded cantonal or communal self-seeking which strikes us as so repulsive in Switzerland, and which all the South German federal republicans wanted to make the rule in Germany in 1849. – Note by Engels to the 1885 edition.]

We have seen how the next upsurge will bring the democrats to power and how they will be forced to propose more or less socialistic measures. It will be asked what measures the workers are to propose in reply. At the beginning, of course, the workers cannot propose any directly communist measures. But the following courses of action are possible:

1. They can force the democrats to make inroads into as many areas of the existing social order as possible, so as to disturb its regular functioning and so that the petty-bourgeois democrats compromise themselves; furthermore, the workers can force the concentration of as many productive forces as possible – means of transport, factories, railways, etc. – in the hands of the state.

2. They must drive the proposals of the democrats to their logical extreme (the democrats will in any case act in a reformist and not a revolutionary manner) and transform these proposals into direct attacks on private property. If, for instance, the petty bourgeoisie propose the purchase of the railways and factories, the workers must demand that these railways and factories simply be confiscated by the state without compensation as the property of reactionaries. If the democrats propose a proportional tax, then the workers must demand a progressive tax; if the democrats themselves propose a moderate progressive tax, then the workers must insist on a tax whose rates rise so steeply that big capital is ruined by it; if the democrats demand the regulation of the state debt, then the workers must demand national bankruptcy. The demands of the workers will thus have to be adjusted according to the measures and concessions of the democrats.

Although the German workers cannot come to power and achieve the realization of their class interests without passing through a protracted revolutionary development, this time they can at least be certain that the first act of the approaching revolutionary drama will coincide with the direct victory of their own class in France and will thereby be accelerated. But they themselves must contribute most to their final victory, by informing themselves of their own class interests, by taking up their independent political position as soon as possible, by not allowing themselves to be misled by the hypocritical phrases of the democratic petty bourgeoisie into doubting for one minute the necessity of an independently organized party of the proletariat. Their battle-cry must be: *The Permanent Revolution.*

Marx & Engels: Address of the Central Committee to the Communist League

In our last circular, delivered to you by the League's emissary, we discussed the position of the workers' party and, in particular, of the League, both at the present moment and in the event of revolution.

The main purpose of this letter is to present a report on the state of the League.

For a while, following the defeats sustained by the revolutionary party last summer, the League's organization almost completely disintegrated. The most active League members involved in the various movements were dispersed, contacts were broken off and addresses could no longer be used; because of this and because of the danger of letters being opened, correspondence became temporarily impossible. The Central Committee was thus condemned to complete inactivity until around the end of last year.

As the immediate after-effects of our defeats gradually passed, it became clear that the revolutionary party needed a strong secret organization throughout Germany. The need for this organization, which led the Central Committee to decide to send an emissary to Germany and Switzerland, also led to an attempt by the Cologne commune to organize the League in Germany itself.

Around the beginning of the year several more or less well-known refugees from the various movements formed an organization in Switzerland which intended to overthrow the governments at the right moment and to keep men at the ready to take over the leadership of the movement and even the government itself. This association did not possess any particular party character; the motley elements which it comprised made this impossible. The members consisted of people from all groups within the movement, from resolute Communists and even former League members to the most faint-hearted petty-bourgeois democrats and former members of the Palatinate government.

In the eyes of the Baden-Palatinate careerists and lesser ambitious figures who were so numerous in Switzerland at this time, this association presented an ideal opportunity for them to advance themselves.

The instructions which this association sent to its agents — and which the Central Committee has in its possession — give just as little cause for confidence. The lack of a definite party standpoint and the attempt to bring all available opposition elements together in a sham association is only badly disguised by a mass of detailed questions concerning the industrial, agricultural, political and military situations in each locality. Numerically, too, the association was extremely weak; according to the complete list of members which we possess, the whole society in Switzerland consisted, at the height of its strength, of barely thirty members. It is significant that workers are hardly represented at all among the membership. From its very beginning, it was an army of officers and N.C.O.'s without any soldiers. Its members include A. Fries and Greiner from the Palatinate, Korner from Elberfeld, Sigel, etc.

They sent two agents to Germany. The first agent, Bruhn, a member of the League, managed by false pretences to persuade certain League members and communes to join the new association for the time being, as they believed it to be the resurrected League. While reporting on the League to the Swiss Central Committee in Zurich, he simultaneously sent us reports on the Swiss association. He cannot have been content with his role as an informer, for while he was still corresponding with us, he wrote outright slanders to the people in Frankfurt, who had been won over to the Swiss association, and he ordered them not to enter into any contacts whatsoever with London. For this he was immediately expelled from the League. Matters in Frankfurt were settled by an emissary from the League. It may be added that Bruhn's activities on behalf of the Swiss Central Committee remained fruitless. The second agent, the student Schurz from Bonn, achieved nothing because, as he wrote to Zurich, he found that all the people of any use were already in the hands of the League. He then suddenly left Germany and is now hanging around Brussels and Paris, where he is being watched by the League. The Central Committee does not see this new association as a danger, particularly as a completely reliable member of the League is on the committee, with instructions to observe and report on the actions and plans of these people, in so far as they operate against the League. Furthermore, we have sent an emissary to Switzerland in order to recruit the people who will be of value to the League, with the help of the aforementioned League member, and in order to organize the League in Switzerland in general. This information is based on fully authentic documents.

Another attempt of a similar nature had already been made earlier by Struve, Sigel and others, at the time that they joined forces in Geneva. These people had no compunction about claiming quite flatly that the association they were attempting to found was the League, nor about using the names of League members for precisely this end. Of course, they deceived nobody with this lie. Their attempt was so fruitless in every respect that the few members of this abortive association who stayed in Switzerland eventually had to join the organization previously mentioned. But the more impotent this coterie became, the more it showed off with pretentious titles like the 'Central Committee of European Democracy' etc. Struve, together with a few other disappointed great men, has continued these attempts here in London. Manifestoes and appeals to join the 'Central Bureau of German Refugees' and the 'Central Committee of European Democracy' have been sent to all parts of Germany, but this time, too, without the least success.

The contacts which this coterie claims to have made with French and other non-German revolutionaries do not exist. Their whole activity is limited to a few petty intrigues among the German refugees here in London, which do not affect the League directly and which are harmless and easy to keep under surveillance. All these attempts have either the same purpose as the League, namely the revolutionary organization of the workers' party, in which case they are undermining the centralization and strength of the party by fragmenting it and are therefore of a decidedly harmful, separatist character, or else they can only serve to misuse the workers' party for purposes which are foreign or straightforwardly hostile to it. Under certain circumstances the workers' party can profitably use other parties and groups for its own purposes, but it must not subordinate itself to any other party. Those people who were in government during the last movement, and used their position only to betray the movement and to crush the workers' party were it tried to operate independently, must be kept at a distance at all costs.

The following is a report on the state of the League:

i. Belgium

The League's organization among the Belgian workers, as it existed in 1846 and 1847, has naturally come to an end, since the leading members were arrested in 1848 and condemned to death, having their sentences commuted to life imprisonment with hard labour. In general, the League in Belgium has lost strength since the February revolution and since most of the members of the German Workers Association were driven out of Brussels. The police measures which have been introduced have prevented its reorganization. Nevertheless one commune in Brussels has carried on throughout; it is still in existence today and is functioning to the best of its ability.

ii. Germany

In this circular the Central Committee intended to submit a special report on the state of the League in Germany. However, this report can not be made at the present time, as the Prussian police are even now investigating an extensive network of contacts in the revolutionary party. This circular, which will reach Germany safely but which, of course, may here and there fall into the hands of the police while being distributed within Germany, must therefore be written so that its contents do not provide them with weapons which could be used against the League. The Central Committee will therefore confine itself, for the time being, to the following remarks:

In Germany the league has its main centres in Cologne, Frankfurt am Main, Hanau, Mainz, Wiesbaden, Hamburg, Schwerin, Berlin, Breslau, Liegnitz, Glogau, Leipzig, Nuremberg, Munich, Bamberg, Wurzburg, Stuttgart and Baden.

The following towns have been chosen as central districts: Hamburg for Schleswig-Holstein; Schwerin for Mecklenburg; Breslau for Silesia; Leipzig for Saxony and Berlin; Nuremberg for Bavaria, Cologne for the Rhineland and Westphalia. The communes in Gottingen, Stuttgart and Brussels will remain in direct contact with the Central Committee for the time being, until they have succeeded in widening their influence to the extent necessary to form new central districts.

A decision will not be made on the position of the League in Baden until the report has been received from the emissary sent there and to Switzerland.

Wherever peasant and agricultural workers' association exist, as in Schleswig-Holstein and Mecklenburg, members of the League have succeeded in exercising a direct influence upon them and, in some cases, in gaining complete control. For the most part, the workers and agricultural workers' associations in Saxony, Franconia, Hesse and Nassau are also under the leadership of the League. The most influential members of the Workers Brotherhood also belong to the League. The Central Committee wishes to point out to all communes and League members that it is of the utmost importance to win influence in the workers', sports, peasants' and agricultural workers' associations, etc. everywhere. It requests the central districts and the communes corresponding directly with the Central Committee to give a special report in their subsequent letters on what has been achieved in this connection.

The emissary to Germany, who as received a vote of commendation from the Central Committee for his activities, has everywhere recruited only the most reliable people into the League and left the expansion of the League to their greater local knowledge. It will depend upon the local situation whether convinced revolutionaries can be enlisted. Where this is not possible a second class of League members must be created for those people who are reliable and make useful revolutionaries but who do not yet understand the full communist implications of the present movement. This second class, to whom the association must be represented as a merely local or regional affair, must remain under the continuous leadership of actual League members and committees. With the help of these further contacts the League's influence on the peasants' and sports associations in particular can be very firmly organized. Detailed arrangements are left to the central districts; the Central Committee hopes to receive their reports on these matters, too, as soon as possible.

One commune has proposed to the Central Committee that a Congress of the League be convened, indeed in German itself. The communes and districts will certainly appreciate that under the present circumstances even regional congresses of the central districts are not everywhere advisable, and that a general Congress of the League at this moment is a sheer impossibility. However, the Central Committee will convene a Congress of the Communist League in a suitable place just as soon as circumstances allow. Prussian Rhineland and Westphalia recently received a visit from an emissary of the Cologne central district. The report on the result of this trip has not yet reached Cologne. We request all central districts to send similar emissaries round their regions and to report on their success as soon as possible. Finally we should like to report that in Schleswig-Holstein, contacts have been established with the army: we are still awaiting the more detailed report on the influence which the League can hope to gain here.

iii. Switzerland

The report of the emissary is still being awaited. It will therefore not be possible to provide more exact information until the next circular.

iv. France

Contacts with the German workers in Besancon and other places in the Jura will be re-established from Switzerland. In Paris Ewerbeck, the League member who has been up till now at the head of the commune there, has announced his resignation from the League, as he considers his literary activities to be more important.

Contact has therefore been interrupted for the present and must be resumed with particular caution, as the Parisians have enlisted a large number of people who are absolutely unfitted for the League and who were formerly even directly opposed to it.

v. England

The London district is the strongest in the whole League. It has earned particular credit by covering single-handedly the League's expenses for several years — in particular those for the journeys of the League's emissaries. It has been strengthened recently by the recruitment of new elements and it continues to lead the German Workers Educational Association here, as well as the more resolute section of the German refugees in England.

The Central Committee is in touch with the decisively revolutionary parties of the French, English and Hungarians by way of members delegated for this purpose.

Of all the parties involved in the French revolution it is in particular the genuine proletarian party headed by Blanqui which has joined us. The delegates of the Blanquist secret society are in regular and official contact with the delegates of the League, to whom they have entrusted important preparatory work for the next revolution.

The leaders of the revolutionary wing of the Chartists are also in regular and close contact with the delegates of the Central Committee. Their journals are being made available to us. The break between this revolutionary, independent workers' party and the faction headed by O'Connor, which tends more towards a policy of reconciliation, has been considerably accelerated by the delegates of the League.

The Central Committee is similarly in contact with the most progressive section of the Hungarian refugees. This party is important because it includes many excellent military experts, who would be at the League's disposal in the event of revolution.

The Central Committee requests the central districts to distribute this letter among their members as soon as possible and to submit their own reports soon. It urges all League members to the most intense activity, especially now that the situation has become so critical that it cannot be long before another revolution breaks out.

Introduction to "The April Theses" and their Presentation

The fortunes of the international socialist movement seemed to change considerably in the seven decades between the appearance of the Communist Manifesto and the October Revolution. On the one hand, its ranks expanded into a well organised mass movement, producing industrialised Germany's largest political party and large organisations in other industrialised states. On the other hand, this produced vested interests within the movement that weakened its militancy and set it on the road to becoming a petit bourgeois force like those denounced by Marx and Engels.

Central to this was the party programme. For Marx and Engels, it was aimed at mobilising the workers and the oppressed to overthrow the capitalist states. For too many of their heirs, it was aimed at attracting recruits to party and trade unions to support the election of deputies to the parliaments of those capitalist states to reform these states piecemeal. While the programme of socialism remained the ultimate aim (the Maximum Programme), the programme of demands drafted to create activists for that end became a set of desirable minimum proposals to be achieved constitutionally. Nor was there, when one such demand was achieved, any attempt to replace it with a more radical one to raise popular consciousness further.

This opportunism tended to be centred on the socialist (now styled Social Democratic) parties' approach to the state. Tactical participation in elections became acceptance of the institutions of capitalist democracy as the means for the workers to achieve state power and for some, socialism in a single state. Old Frederick Engels criticised the German Social Democrats' draft programme for adapting thus to their country's constitution.2. The Austrians went further in accepting the policies of their state, refusing to condemn its incorporation of Bosnia-Herzegovina.

In Russia, the obvious brutality of the imperial regime, and the relative youth of the radicalising working-class tended to act against such obvious departures from Marxism. Though some early socialists came to believe in peaceful change, they went further and became liberals. The Marxist mainstream was agreed that the state would have to be overthrown for socialism to come to their country. The question was how this was to be done in a country where the urban workers were a minority and the peasantry the vast majority. Led by Lenin, the majority (Bolsheviks) declared the proletariat, backed by the peasants, would achieve state power, the minority (Mensheviks) maintained the bourgeoisie would make their revolution and introduce the democracy necessary for the workers' movement to flourish. Only

Trotsky asserted that the workers and peasants could not only overthrow the regime but that their government had to go beyond socialism's minimum demands.

The Bolshevik-Menshevik division produced initially some interesting conclusions. When revolution occurred in 1905, Trotsky saw the councils (Soviets) established by the mobilising workers as the basis for the form of a new revolutionary state. The Bolsheviks had to be told by Lenin to participate in them, as the source of the proletarian-peasant dictatorship in Russian bourgeois democracy4 leaving open a final bourgeois constitutional settlement. The Mensheviks were quicker to join the soviets, but saw them only as local appendages to the bourgeois power seizure.

The revolution failed and the First World War came before it could be repeated. However, the war itself helped escalate trends leading to revolution. In March (Russian style: February) 1917, the Petrograd and Moscow workers, including the local railway workers rebelled, formed new soviets and forced the Tsar to abdicate.

The Bolsheviks had been targeted for repression by the fallen regime and were too weak to take a leading role in the new councils. These were led by Mensheviks and non-Marxist Social Revolutionaries who endorsed the seizure of state power by a group of liberal politicians who formed a Provisional Government to rule Russia and prepare for a Constituent Assembly. For the Mensheviks, this government would complete the bourgeois revolution to enable social democracy to take state power.

After a revolutionary start, the Bolsheviks in Petrograd accepted this in practice if not in theory. While not confident about the new regime they assumed its endorsement by the Petrograd Soviet made it the democratic dictatorship and acted to strengthen pressure on it and gain prestige as the best builders for the Constituent Assembly. This meant playing down criticisms of the

Government as such, even on the war that that government was pledged to continue to victory.

In exile, Lenin opposed this, insisting that the government had usurped power from the soviets and that it would not deliver 'peace, bread and full freedom'. On his return, in April, he broadened his demands in the April Theses republished here.

These theses and their justifications moved the Bolshevik programme closer to the position of Trotsky. Demands that had been traditionally bourgeois democratic were merged with those the bourgeoisie could not tolerate, not least, the removal of sovereignty from the government to the Soviets. The land reform was to be centred on co-operative farming rather than division of farmland (this would prove impossible for the actual revolutionary regime), banks would be nationalised and production directed by the Soviet power. Above all, the war had to be ended at any cost, even unilaterally. The government had to be exposed as unable deliver on its expectations because it was capitalist. Nonetheless, in presenting his theses, Lenin was careful to emphasise that the Bolshevik alternative would 'not "introduce" socialism [that is, a socialist society]..., but, rather, practice it [as policies, many of which were being used by and for capitalism]', a distinction ignored by most of his self-styled heirs. To objections that the workers and peasants were not ready for such measures, Lenin emphasised the need for patient propaganda for necessary demands. This was the programme that made the October Revolution.

In power, the Bolsheviks tried to operate on these lines. Indeed the fifth thesis is particularly saddening, with its emphasis on the abolition of police, army and bureaucracy, of arming the population and electing all officials, when it is remembered what happened to the Soviet Union. Were these demands mistaken?

Certainly, the strategy involved mistakes, but less in the specific demands than in the optimism of the Bolsheviks and their fellow-thinkers. They under-estimated their opponents in Russia and outside. Within Russia, the victorious revolutionaries set free those who had opposed them in arms, enabling them to form the nucleus of their opponents in a particularly vicious and wasteful civil war that lasted until 1922. Outside Russia, those who wanted seriously to copy the Bolsheviks were still few in number and, more importantly, disorganised compared to their opponents in and outside their countries' labour movements. Attempts, great and little, to spread the revolution beyond Russia were crushed by national bourgeoisies, supported, with various degrees of enthusiasm by the reformist labour leaders. Such defeats created the circumstances for Russia's revolutionaries to turn their perspectives inward, to seek to build a socialist society in their own single country, and to maintain themselves in this task by strengthening and expanding the repressive apparatus that had been required during the civil war. After decades, this apparatus would be partially dismantled, but only after it had destroyed the Russian workers' potential for full power, and, with it, much of the potential for such power outside Russia.

For all that, the Russian revolution, and its programme remains, like a bigger and more developed Paris Commune, a shining light for the world's workers. The only thing that the reformists have to offer is the post-1945 British welfare state, based on a far richer supply of surplus wealth, and itself looking distinctly ragged after eleven years of continuous rule by the heirs of its founders. Lenin and Trotsky made mistakes, but they dared lead the workers to take state power. Both facts should be remembered and analysed. In the balance, the daring outweighs the errors.

The final form of the 'April Theses' and the 'Letters on Tactics' were published as a pamphlet by the Bolsheviks shortly after they first appeared. In this form, they were republished in many translations by Progress Publishers over subsequent years. For this edition, the editor has added the stenographic report of Lenin's original presentation of his Theses to the Meeting of Bolshevik Delegates to the All-Russia Conference of Soviets of Workers' and Soldiers' Deputies immediately after his return in April, and his Notes for his defence of the Theses, as both add points that were not considered as important at the time as they are today.

Lenin: Report at a meeting of Bolshevik delegates to the All-Russia Conference of Soviets of Workers' and Soldiers' Deputies April 4 (17), 1917

I have put down a few theses on which I will make some comments. For lack of time I was unable to present a circumstantial and systematic report[2].

The basic question is the attitude to the war. The main thing that comes to the fore, when you read about Russia and see what goes on here, is the victory of defencism, the victory of the traitors to socialism, the deception of the masses by the bourgeoisie. What

---

[2] *All-Russia Conference of Party Workers* (March Conference) was timed by the Russian Bureau of the R.S.D.L.P. C.C. for the All-Russia Conference of Soviets of Workers' and Soldiers' Deputies and opened on March 27 (April 9), 1917. On its agenda were: attitude to the war, attitude to the Provisional Government, organisation of revolutionary forces, etc. The meeting of April 4 (17) at which Lenin gave his report was held in the Taurida Palace. Lenin explained his April Theses and quoted them in part. The text of his speech is reproduced from secretarial notes containing lacunae indicated with dots, apart from some places of the notes which are not quite clear.

All-Russia Conference of Soviets of Workers' and Soldiers' Deputies, called by the Executive Committee of the Petrograd Soviet, was held at Petrograd from March 29 to April 3 (April 11 to 16), 1917. It was attended by representatives of the Petrograd Soviet and 82 local Soviets, and also of army units at the front and in the rear. It discussed the questions of the war, the attitude to the Provisional Government, the Constituent Assembly, land, food, and other problems. The Conference, which was dominated by Mensheviks and S.R.s, took the attitude of "revolutionary defencism" (325 against 57) and adopted a decision to support the bourgeois Provisional Government and also to call an international socialist conference on the question of withdrawal from the war. G. V. Plekhanov made two speeches in a spirit of social-patriotism. There were interruptions from the defencist majority when the Bolshevik P. I. Starostin called for an end to the war. The Conference added 16 members to the Executive Committee of the Petrograd Soviet, including six from the Army and Navy.

strikes one is that here in Russia the socialist movement is in the same state as in other countries: defencism, "defence of the fatherland". The difference is that nowhere is there such freedom as here and therefore we have a special responsibility to the whole international proletariat. The new government is as imperialist as the previous one; it is imperialist through and through, despite its promise of a republic.

"I. In our attitude towards the war, which under the new government of Lvov and Co. unquestionably remains on Russia's part a predatory imperialist war owing to the capitalist nature of that government, not the slightest concession to 'revolutionary defencism' is permissible.

"The class-conscious proletariat can give its consent to a revolutionary war, which would really justify revolutionary defencism, only on condition: a) that power passes to the proletariat and the poorest sections of the peasants aligned with the proletariat; b) that all annexations are renounced in deed and not in word; c) that a complete break is effected in actual fact with all capitalist interests.

"In view of the undoubted honesty of those broad sections of the mass believers in revolutionary defencism who accept the war only as a necessity, and not as a means of conquest, in view of the fact that they are being deceived by the bourgeoisie, it is necessary with particular thoroughness, persistence and patience to explain their error to them, to explain the inseparable connection existing between capital and the imperialist war, and to prove that without overthrowing capital it is impossible to end the war by a truly democratic peace, a peace not imposed by violence.

"The most widespread campaign for this view must be organised in the army at the front.

"Fraternisation."

We cannot allow the slightest concession to defencism in our attitude to the war even under the new government, which remains imperialist. The masses take a practical and not a theoretical view of things. They say: "I want to defend the fatherland, not to seize other peoples' lands." When can a war be considered your own? When annexations are completely renounced.

The masses take a practical and not a theoretical approach to the question. We make the mistake of taking the theoretical approach. A class-conscious proletarian can agree to a revolutionary war, which really does justify revolutionary defencism. The practical approach is the only possible one with representatives of the mass of the soldiers. We are not pacifists in any sense. But the main question is: which class is carrying on the war? The class of capitalists, linked with the banks, cannot wage any kind of war except an imperialist one. The working class can. Steklov and Chkheidze have forgotten everything. When you read the resolution of the Soviet of Workers' Deputies, you are amazed that people calling themselves socialists could adopt such a resolution.[6]

What is specific in Russia is the extremely rapid transition from savage violence to the most subtle deception. The main condition is *renunciation of annexations not in words*, but in deeds. *Rech* howls at *Sotsial-Demokrat*'s statement that the integration of Courland with Russia is annexation. But annexation is the integration of any country with distinct national peculiarities; it is any integration of a nation against its will, irrespective of whether it differs in language, if it feels itself to be another people. This is a prejudice of the Great Russians which has been fostered for centuries.

The war can be ended only by a clean break with international capital. The war was engendered not by individuals but by international finance capital. It is no easy thing to break with international capital, but neither is it an easy thing to end the war. It is childishness and naïveté to expect one side alone to end the war.... Zimmerwald, Kienthal[3].... We have a greater obligation than anyone else to safeguard the honour of international socialism. The difficulty of approach....

In view of the undoubted existence of a defencist mood among the masses, who recognise the war *only of necessity* and not for the sake of conquest, we must explain to them most circumstantially, persistently and patiently that the war cannot be ended in a non-rapacious peace unless capital is overthrown. This idea must be spread far and wide. The soldiers want a concrete answer: how to end the war. But it is political fraud to promise the people that we can end the war only by the goodwill of individual persons. The masses must be forewarned. A revolution is a difficult thing. It is impossible to avoid mistakes. Our mistake is that we (have not exposed?) revolutionary defencism to the full. Revolutionary defencism is betrayal of socialism. We cannot confine ourselves.... We must admit our mistake. What is to be done? To explain. How to

---

[3] A reference to the international socialist conferences at Zimmerwald and Kienthal.

present... who doesn't know what socialism is.... We are not charlatans. We must base ourselves only on the political consciousness of the masses. Even if we have to remain in a minority—let it be so. It is worth while giving up our leading position for a time; we should not be afraid of remaining in a minority. When the masses say they don't want conquest, I believe them. When Guchkov and Lvov say they don't want conquest, they are swindlers. When the worker says that he wants to defend the country, he voices the oppressed man's instinct.

"II. The specific feature of the present situation in Russia is that the country is passing from the first stage of the revolution— which, owing to the insufficient class— consciousness and organisation of the proletariat, placed power in the hands of the bourgeoisie—to the second stage, which must place power in the hands of the proletariat and the poorest sections of the peasants.

"This transition is characterised, on the one hand, by a maximum of legally recognised rights (Russia is now the freest of all the belligerent countries in the world); on the other, by the absence of violence towards the masses, and, finally, by their unreasoning trust in the government of capitalists, those worst enemies of peace and socialism.

"This peculiar situation demands of us an ability to adapt ourselves to the special conditions of Party work among unprecedentedly large masses of proletarians who have just awakened to political life."

Why didn't they take power? Steklov says: for this reason and that. This is nonsense. The fact is that the proletariat is not organised and class-conscious enough. This must be admitted; material strength is in the hands of the proletariat, but the bourgeoisie turned out to be prepared and class-conscious. This is a monstrous fact, but it should be frankly and openly admitted, and the people should be told that they didn't take power because they were unorganised and not conscious enough.... The ruin of millions, the death of millions. The most advanced countries are on the brink of disaster, and they will therefore be faced with the question....

The transition from the first stage to the second—the transfer of power to the proletariat and the peasantry—is characterised, on the one hand, by the maximum of legality (Russia today is the freest and most progressive country in the world) and, on the other, by an attitude of blind trust on the part of the masses in the government. Even our Bolsheviks show some trust in the government. This can be explained only by the intoxication of the revolution. It is the death of socialism. You comrades have a trusting attitude to the government. If that is so, our paths diverge. I prefer to remain in a minority. One Liebknecht is worth more than 110 defencists of the Steklov and Chkheidze type. If you sympathise with Liebknecht and stretch out even a finger (to the defencists), it will be betrayal of international socialism. If we break away from those people ... everyone who is oppressed will come to us, because the war will lead him to us; he has no other way out.

The people should be spoken to without Latin words, in clear and simple terms. They have the right ...—we must adapt ourselves ... make the change, but it is essential. Our line will prove to be the correct one.

"III. No support for the Provisional Government; the utter falsity of all its promises should be made clear, particularly of those relating to the renunciation of annexations. Exposure in place of the impermissible, illusion-breeding 'demand' that this government, a government of capitalists, should cease to be an imperialist government. "

Pravda demands of the *government* that it should renounce annexations. To demand of a government of capitalists that it should renounce annexations is nonsense, a crying mockery of....

From the scientific standpoint this is such gross deception which all the international proletariat, all.... It is time to admit our mistake. We've had enough of greetings and resolutions, it is time to act. We must get down to a sober, business-like....

"IV. Recognition of the fact that in most of the Soviets of Workers' Deputies our Party is in a minority, so far a small minority, as against a bloc of all *the petty-bourgeois opportunist elements, from the Popular Socialists* [4] *and the Socialist-Revolutionaries down to the Organising Committee (Chkheidze, Tsereteli, etc.), Steklov, etc., etc., who have yielded to the influence of the bourgeoisie and spread that influence among the proletariat.*

---

[4] Members of a petty-bourgeois Trudovik Popular Socialist Party formed in 1906 by Right-wingers of the Socialist-Revolutionary Party (S.R.). They sided with the Cadets; Lenin called them "Social-Cadets", "philistine opportunists", "S.R. Mensheviks", vacillating between the S.R.s and the Cadets. He said, the party "differs very little from the Cadets, for it deletes from its programme both republicanism and the demand for all the land" = (see *Works*, Vol. 11, p. 228). Among the party's leaders were A. V. Peshekhonov, N. F. Annensky and V. A. Myakotin.

"The masses must be made to see that the Soviets of Workers' Deputies are the only possible *form of revolutionary government, and that therefore our task is, as long as* this *government yields to the influence of the bourgeoisie, to present a patient, systematic, and persistent* explanation *of the errors of their tactics, an explanation especially adapted to the practical needs of the masses.*

"As long as we are in the minority we carry on the work of criticising and exposing errors and at the same time we preach the necessity of transferring the entire state power to the Soviets of Workers' Deputies, so that the people may overcome their mistakes by experience."

We Bolsheviks are in the habit of taking the line of maximum revolutionism. But that is not enough. We must sort things out.

The Soviet of Workers' Deputies is the real government. To think otherwise is to fall into anarchism. It is a recognised fact that in the Soviet of Workers' Deputies our Party is in a minority. We must explain to the masses that the Soviet of Workers' Deputies is the only possible government, a government without parallel in the world, except for the Commune. What if a majority of the Soviet of Workers' Deputies takes the defencist stand? That cannot be helped. It remains for us to explain, patiently, persistently, systematically, the erroneous nature of their tactics.

So long as we are in a minority, we carry on the work of criticism, in order to open the people's eyes to the deception. We don't want the masses to take our word for it. We are not charlatans. We want the masses to overcome their mistakes through *experience.*

The manifesto of the Soviet of Workers' Deputies contains not a word imbued with class-consciousness. It's all talk! Talk, flattery of the revolutionary people, is the only thing that has ruined all revolutions. The whole of Marxism teaches us not to succumb to revolutionary phrases, particularly at a time when they have the greatest currency.

"V. Not a parliamentary republic—to return to a parliamentary republic from the Soviets of Workers' Deputies would be a retrograde step—but a republic of Soviets of Workers', Agricultural Labourers' and Peasants' Deputies throughout the country, from top to bottom.

"Abolition of the police, the army and the bureaucracy.[5]

---

[5] i.e., the standing army to be replaced by the arming of the whole people.

"The salaries of all officials, all of whom are elective and displaceable at any time, not to exceed the average wage of a competent worker."

This is the lesson of the French Commune, which Kautsky forgot and which the workers teach us in 1905 and 1917. The experience of these years teaches us that we must not allow the police and the old army to be restored.

The programme should be changed, it is out of date. The Soviet of Workers' and Soldiers' Deputies is a step to socialism. There must be no police, no army, no officialdom. The convocation of the Constituent Assembly—but by whom? Resolutions are written only to be shelved or sat on. I should be glad to have the Constituent Assembly convened tomorrow, but it is naïve to believe that Guchkov will call it. All the chatter about forcing the Provisional Government to call the Constituent Assembly is empty talk, a pack of lies. Revolutions were made, but the police stayed on, revolutions were made, but all the officials, etc., stayed on. That was why the revolutions foundered. The Soviet of Workers' Deputies is the only government which can call that assembly. We all seized upon the Soviets of Workers' Deputies, but have failed to understand them. From this form we are dragging back to the International, which is trailing behind the bourgeoisie.

A bourgeois republic cannot solve the problem (of the war), because it can be solved only on an international scale. We don't promise liberation ... but we say that it is possible only in this form (Soviet of Workers' and Soldiers' Deputies). No government except the Soviet of Workers' and Agricultural Labourers' Deputies. If you talk about the Commune, they won't understand. But if you say, there is the Soviet of Workers' and Agricultural Labourers' Deputies instead of the police, learn to govern— no one can interfere with us—(that they will understand).

No books will ever teach you the art of government. Learning to govern is a matter of trial and error.

"VI. The weight of emphasis in the agrarian programme to be shifted to the Soviets of Agricultural Labourers' Deputies.

"Confiscation of all landed estates.

"Nationalisation of all lands in the country, the land to be disposed of by the local Soviets of Agricultural Labourers' and Peasants' Deputies. The organisation of separate Soviets of Deputies of Poor Peasants. The setting up of a model farm on each of the large estates (ranging in size from 100 to 300 dessiatines, according to local and other conditions and to the decisions of the

local bodies) under the control of the Soviets of Agricultural Labourers' Deputies and for the public account."

What is the peasantry? We don't know, there are no statistics, but we do know that it is a force.

If they take the land, you can be sure that they won't give it back to you, they won't ask us. The pivot, the centre of gravity of the programme has shifted, and is the Soviets of Agricultural Labourers' Deputies. If the Russian peasant doesn't settle the revolution, the German worker will.

The Tambov muzhik....

The first dessiatine cost free, the second, for 1 ruble, the third, for 2 rubles. We shall take over the land, and the landowner will never be able to take it back.

Communal farming

It is necessary to organise separate Soviets of Deputies from the poor peasants. There is the rich muzhik, and there is the labourer. Even if you give him land, he won't set up a farm. The large estates should be turned into model farms run on social lines, with management by the Soviets of Agricultural Labourers' Deputies.

There are large estates.

"VII. The immediate amalgamation of all banks in the country into a single national bank, and the institution of control over it by the Soviet of Workers' Deputies."

The bank is "a form of social book-keeping" (Marx). War teaches economy; everyone knows that the banks sap the strength of the people. The banks are the nerve, the focus of the national economy. We cannot take hold of the banks, but we advocate their amalgamation under the control of the Soviet of Workers' Deputies.

"VIII. It is not our immediate task to 'introduce' socialism, but only to bring social production and the distribution of products at once under the control of the Soviets of Workers' Deputies."

Practice and the revolution tend to push the Constituent Assembly into the background. The important thing about laws is not that they are put down on paper, but who carries them out. The dictatorship of the proletariat is there, but people don't know how to work it. Capitalism has developed into state capitalism.... Marx ... only that which has matured in practice....

"IX. Party tasks:

(a) Immediate convocation of a Party congress.

(b) Amendment of the Party Programme, mainly:

1) On the question of imperialism and the imperialist war;

2) On our attitude towards the state and our demand for a "commune state"[6];

3) Amendment of our out-of-date minimum programme.

(c) Change of the Party's name.[7]

"X. A new International.

"We must take the initiative in creating a revolutionary International, an International against the social– chauvinists *and against the 'Centre'.[8]"*

General conclusion

The Soviet of Workers' Deputies has been created, it enjoys vast influence. All instinctively sympathise with it. This institution combines far more revolutionary thought than all the *revolutionary phrases.* If the Soviet of Workers' Deputies succeeds in taking government into its own hands, the cause of liberty is assured. You may write the most ideal laws, but who will put them into effect? The same officials, but they are tied up with the bourgeoisie.

It is not "introduce socialism" that we ought to tell the masses, but put it into effect (?). Capitalism has gone ahead; war capitalism is different from that which existed before the war.

On the basis of our tactical conclusions we must go on to practical steps. A Party congress must be called at once and the Programme revised. A great deal in it is out of date. The minimum programme must be changed.

I personally propose that we change the name of our Party and call it the *Communist Party.* The people will understand the name of "Communist". Most of the official Social-Democrats have committed treason, they have betrayed socialism.... Liebknecht is the one Social– Democrat.... You are afraid of betraying old

---

[6] That is, a state of which the Paris Commune was the prototype.

[7] We must call ourselves the *Communist Party*, instead of "Social-Democratic", for the official Social-Democrat leaders *throughout* the world have betrayed socialism and have gone over to the bourgeoisie (the "defencists" and wavering "Kautskians").—*Lenin*

[8] "Centre" is the name given among international Social-Democrats to the trend which wavers between the chauvinists (=the "defencists") and the internationalists, namely, Kautsky and Co. in Germany; Longuet and Co. in France; Chkheidze and Co. in Russia; Turati and Co. in Italy; MacDonald and Co. in Britain, etc.—*Lenin*

recollections. But if you want to change your underwear you must take off your dirty shirt and put on a clean one. Why throw out the experience of world-wide struggle? Most of the Social-Democrats throughout the world have betrayed socialism, and have sided with their governments (Scheidemann, Plekhanov, Guesde). What is to be done to make Scheidemann agree?... This point of view spells ruin for socialism. It would be deception to send a radio telegram to Scheidemann about ending the war....

The term "Social-Democracy" is inexact. Don't cling to an old word which has become rotten through and through. If you want to build a new party ... and all the oppressed will come to you.

The Centre prevailed at Zimmerwald and Kienthal.... *Rabochaya Gazeta*. We shall prove to you that the whole of experience has shown.... We declare that we have formed a Left wing and have broken with the Centre. Either you speak about the International, then carry out..., or you....

The Left Zimmerwald trend exists in all the countries of the world. The masses must realise that socialism has split throughout the world. The defencists have renounced socialism. Liebknecht alone.... The future is with him.

I have heard that there is a tendency in Russia towards unification, towards unity with the defencists. This is betrayal of socialism. I think it is better to remain alone, like Liebknecht: one against 110.

Lenin: Notes for an Article or Speech in Defence of the April Theses

(1) Economic debacle is imminent. Therefore removal of the bourgeoisie is a mistake.

(This is the conclusion of the bourgeoisie. The more imminent the debacle, the more essential is it that the bourgeoisie be removed.)

(2) Proletariat is unorganised, weak, lacking class-consciousness.

(True. Therefore, the whole task is to fight those *petty-bourgeois* leaders, the so-called Social-Democrats—Chkheidze, Tsereteli, Steklov—who lull the masses, encourage them to put their trust in the bourgeoisie.

Not unity with these petty bourgeois—Chkheidze, Steklov, Tsereteli—but *utter defeat* of these Social-Democrats, who are ruining the revolution of the proletariat.)

(3) Revolution is bourgeois at the present stage. Therefore no need for "socialist experiment".

(This argument is an out-and-out bourgeois argument. No one talks about a "socialist experiment" The concrete Marxist proposition requires that institutions now as well as classes be taken into account.)

Stranglers of the revolution, by honeyed phrases—Chkheidze, Tsereteli, Steklov—are dragging the revolution back, *away from* the Soviets of Workers' Deputies *towards* the undivided sway of the bourgeoisie, towards the usual bourgeois parliamentary republic.

We must ably, carefully, clear people's minds and lead the proletariat and poor peasantry *forward*, away from "dual power" *towards the full power* of the Soviets of Workers' Deputies, and this is the commune in Marx's sense, in the sense of the experience of 1871.

The question is not how fast to move, but where to move.

The question is not whether the workers are prepared, but *how* and *for what* they should be prepared.

Since the manifestos and appeals of the Soviet of Workers' Deputies on the war, etc., are sheer petty-bourgeois humbug designed merely to lull the people to sleep, it is our business above all, as I have said, to clear people's minds, to rid the masses of the *bourgeois* influence of Chkheidze, Steklov, Tsereteli and Co.

The "revolutionary defencism" of the Soviet of Workers Deputies, i.e., of Chkheidze, Tsereteli and Steklov, is a chauvinist trend a hundred times more harmful for being cloaked in honeyed phrases, an *attempt* to reconcile the masses with the Provisional Revolutionary Government.

The dull, unenlightened masses duped by Chkheidze, Tsereteli, Steklov and Co. do not realise that the war is a continuation of policy, that wars are waged by *governments*.

It must be made clear that the "people" can stop the war or change its character only by changing the *class character* of the government.

Lenin: The Tasks of the Proletariat in the Present Revolution

I did not arrive in Petrograd until the night of April 3, and therefore at the meeting on April 4, I could, of course, deliver the report on the tasks of the revolutionary proletariat only on my own behalf, and with reservations as to insufficient preparation.

The only thing I could do to make things easier for myself—and for *honest* opponents—was to prepare the theses *in writing*. I read them out, and gave the text to Comrade Tsereteli. I read them *twice* very slowly: first at a meeting of Bolsheviks and then at a meeting of both Bolsheviks and Mensheviks.

I publish these personal theses of mine with only the briefest explanatory notes, which were developed in far greater detail in the report.

Theses

1) In our attitude towards the war, which under the new [provisional] government of Lvov and Co. unquestionably remains on Russia's part a predatory imperialist war owing to the capitalist nature of that government, not the slightest concession to "revolutionary defencism" is permissible.

The class-conscious proletariat can give its consent to a revolutionary war, which would really justify revolutionary defencism, only on condition: (a) that the power pass to the proletariat and the poorest sections of the peasants aligned with the proletariat; (b) that all annexations be renounced in deed and not in word; (c) that a complete break be effected in actual fact with all capitalist interests.

In view of the undoubted honesty of those broad sections of the mass believers in revolutionary defencism who accept the war only as a necessity, and not as a means of conquest, in view of the fact that they are being deceived by the bourgeoisie, it is necessary with particular thoroughness, persistence and patience to explain their error to them, to explain the inseparable connection existing between capital and the imperialist war, and to prove that without overthrowing capital *it is impossible* to end the war by a truly democratic peace, a peace not imposed by violence.

The most widespread campaign for this view must be organised in the army at the front.

Fraternisation.

2) The specific feature of the present situation in Russia is that the country is *passing* from the first stage of the revolution—which, owing to the insufficient class-consciousness and organisation of the proletariat, placed power in the hands of the bourgeoisie—to its *second stage*, which must place power in the hands of the proletariat and the poorest sections of the peasants.

This transition is characterised, on the one hand, by a maximum of legally recognised rights (Russia is *now* the freest of all the belligerent countries in the world); on the other, by the absence of violence towards the masses, and, finally, by their unreasoning trust in the government of capitalists, those worst enemies of peace and socialism.

This peculiar situation demands of us an ability to adapt ourselves to the *special* conditions of Party work among unprecedentedly large masses of proletarians who have just awakened to political life.

3) No support for the Provisional Government; the utter falsity of all its promises should be made clear, particularly of those relating to the renunciation of annexations. Exposure in place of the impermissible, illusion-breeding "demand" that *this* government, a government of capitalists, should *cease* to be an imperialist government.

4) Recognition of the fact that in most of the Soviets of Workers' Deputies our Party is in a minority, so far a small minority, as against a *bloc of all* the petty-bourgeois opportunist elements, from the Popular Socialists and the Socialist-Revolutionaries down to the Organising Committee (Chkheidze, Tsereteli, etc.), Steklov, etc., etc., who have yielded to the influence of the bourgeoisie and spread that influence among the proletariat.

The masses must be made to see that the Soviets of Workers' Deputies are the *only possible* form of revolutionary government, and that therefore our task is, as long as *this* government yields to the influence of the bourgeoisie, to present a patient, systematic, and persistent explanation of the errors of their tactics, an *explanation* especially adapted to the practical needs of the masses.

As long as we are in the minority we carry on the work of criticising and exposing errors and at the same time we preach the necessity of transferring the entire state power to the Soviets of Workers' Deputies, so that the people may overcome their mistakes by experience.

5) Not a parliamentary republic—to return to a parliamentary republic from the Soviets of Workers' Deputies would be a

retrograde step—but a republic of Soviets of Workers', Agricultural Labourers' and Peasants' Deputies throughout the country, from top to bottom.

Abolition of the police, the army and the bureaucracy.

The salaries of all officials, all of whom are elective and displaceable at any time, not to exceed the average wage of a competent worker.

6) The weight of emphasis in the agrarian programme to be shifted to the Soviets of Agricultural Labourers' Deputies.

Confiscation of all landed estates.

Nationalisation of *all* lands in the country, the land to be disposed of by the local Soviets of Agricultural Labourers' and Peasants' Deputies. The organisation of separate Soviets of Deputies of Poor Peasants. The setting up of a model farm on each of the large estates (ranging in size from 100 to 300 dessiatines, according to local and other conditions, and to the decisions of the local bodies) under the control of the Soviets of Agricultural Labourers' Deputies and for the public account.

7) The immediate union of all banks in the country into a single national bank, and the institution of control over it by the Soviet of Workers' Deputies.

8) It is not our *immediate* task to "introduce" socialism, but only to bring social production and the distribution of products at once under the *control* of the Soviets of Workers' Deputies.

9) Party tasks:

(a) Immediate convocation of a Party congress;

(b) Alteration of the Party Programme, mainly:

(1) On the question of imperialism and the imperialist war,

(2) On our attitude towards the state and *our* demand for a "commune state";

(3) Amendment of our out-of-date minimum programme;

(c) Change of the Party's name.

10. A new International.

We must take the initiative in creating a revolutionary International, an International against the *social-chauvinists* and against the "Centre".

In order that the reader may understand why I had especially to emphasise as a rare exception the "case" of honest opponents, I invite him to compare the above theses with the following objection by Mr. Goldenberg: Lenin, he said, "has planted the banner of civil war in the midst of revolutionary democracy" (quoted in No. 5 of Mr. Plekhanov's *Yedinstvo*).

Isn't it a gem?

I write, announce and elaborately explain: "In view of the undoubted honesty of those *broad* sections of the *mass* believers in revolutionary defencism ... in view of the fact that they are being deceived by the bourgeoisie, it is necessary with *particular* thoroughness, persistence and *patience* to explain their error to them...."

Yet the bourgeois gentlemen who call themselves Social-Democrats, who *do not* belong either to the *broad* sections or to the *mass* believers in defencism, with serene brow present my views thus: "The banner[!] of civil war" (of which there is not a word in the theses and not a word in my speech!) has been planted(!) "in the midst [!!] of revolutionary democracy...".

What does this mean? In what way does this differ from riot-inciting agitation, from *Russkaya Volya*?

I write, announce and elaborately explain: "The Soviets of Workers' Deputies are the *only possible* form of revolutionary government, and therefore our task is to present a patient, systematic, and persistent *explanation* of the errors of their tactics, an explanation especially adapted to the practical needs of the masses."

Yet opponents of a certain brand present my views as a call to "civil war in the midst of revolutionary democracy"!

I attacked the Provisional Government for *not* having appointed an early date or any date at all, for the convocation of the Constituent Assembly, and for confining itself to promises. I argued that *without* the Soviets of Workers' and Soldiers' Deputies the convocation of the Constituent Assembly is not guaranteed and its success is impossible.

And the view is attributed to me that I am opposed to the speedy convocation of the Constituent Assembly!

I would call this "raving", had not decades of political struggle taught me to regard honesty in opponents as a rare exception.

Mr. Plekhanov in his paper called my speech "raving". Very good, Mr. Plekhanov! But look how awkward, uncouth and slow-witted you are in your polemics. If I delivered a raving speech for two hours, how is it that an audience of hundreds tolerated this "raving"? Further, why does your paper devote a whole column to an account of the "raving"? Inconsistent, highly inconsistent!

It is, of course, much easier to shout, abuse, and howl than to attempt to relate, to explain, to recall *what* Marx and Engels said in 1871, 1872 and 1875 about the experience of the Paris Commune and about the *kind* of state the proletariat needs. [See: The Civil War in France and Critique of the Gotha Programme]

Ex-Marxist Mr. Plekhanov evidently does not care to recall Marxism.

I quoted the words of Rosa Luxemburg, who on August 4, 1914, called *German* Social-Democracy a "stinking corpse". And the Plekhanovs, Goldenbergs and Co. feel "offended". On whose behalf? On behalf of the *German* chauvinists, because they were called chauvinists!

They have got themselves in a mess, these poor Russian social-chauvinists—socialists in word and chauvinists in deed.

Lenin: Letters on Tactics

Foreword

On April 4, 1917, I had occasion to make a report on the subject indicated in the title, first, at a meeting of Bolsheviks in Petrograd. These were delegates to the All-Russia Conference of Soviets of Workers' and Soldiers' Deputies, who had to leave for their homes and therefore could not allow me to postpone it. After the meeting, the chairman, Comrade G. Zinoviev, asked me on behalf of the whole assembly to repeat my report immediately at a joint meeting of Bolshevik and Menshevik delegates, who wished to discuss the question of unifying the Russian Social-Democratic Labour Party.

Difficult though it was for me immediately to repeat my report, I felt that I had no right to refuse once this was demanded of me by *my comrades-in-ideas* as well as by the Mensheviks, who, because of their impending departure, really could not grant me a delay.

In making my report, I read the theses which were published in No. 26 of Pravda, on April 7, 1917.

Both the theses and my report gave rise to differences of opinion among the Bolsheviks themselves and the editors of *Pravda*. After a number of consultations, we unanimously concluded that it would be advisable *openly* to discuss our differences, and thus provide material for the All-Russia Conference of our Party (the Russian Social-Democratic Labour Party, united under the Central Committee) which is to meet in Petrograd on April 20, 1917.

Complying with this decision concerning a discussion, I am publishing the following *letters* in which I do not claim to have made an *exhaustive* study of the question, but wish merely to outline the principal arguments, which are especially essential for the *practical* tasks of the working-class movement.

First Letter Assessment of the Present Situation

Marxism requires of us a strictly exact and objectively verifiable analysis of the relations of classes and of the concrete features peculiar to each historical situation. We Bolsheviks have always tried to meet this requirement, which is absolutely essential for giving a scientific foundation to policy.

"Our theory is not a dogma, but a guide to action,"[9] Marx and Engels always said, rightly ridiculing the mere memorising and repetition of "formulas", that at best are capable only of marking out *general* tasks, which are necessarily modifiable by the *concrete* economic and political conditions of each particular *period* of the historical process.

What, then, are the clearly established objective *facts* which the party of the revolutionary proletariat must now be guided by in defining the tasks and forms of its activity?

Both in my first *Letter From Afar* ("The First Stage of the First Revolution") published in *Pravda* Nos. 14 and 15, March 21 and 22, *1917*, and in my theses, I define "the specific feature of the present situation in Russia" as a period of *transition* from the first stage of the revolution to the second. I therefore considered the basic slogan, the "task of the day" at *this* moment to be: "Workers, you have performed miracles of proletarian heroism, the heroism of the people, in the civil war against tsarism. You must perform miracles of organisation, organisation of the proletariat and of the whole people, to prepare the way for your victory in the second stage of the revolution" *(Pravda* No. 15).

What, then, is the first stage?

It is the passing of state power to the bourgeoisie.

Before the February-March revolution of *1917,* state power in Russia was in the hands of one old class, namely, the feudal landed nobility, headed by Nicholas Romanov.

After the revolution, the power is in the hands of a *different* class, a new class, namely, the *bourgeoisie.*

The passing of state power from one *class* to another is the first, the principal, the basic sign of a *revolution,* both in the strictly scientific and in the practical political meaning of that term.

To this extent, the bourgeois, or the bourgeois-democratic, revolution in Russia is *completed.*

---

[9] Quoted from Engels's letter to F. A. Serge dated November 29, 1886.

But at this point we hear a clamour of protest from people who readily call themselves "old Bolsheviks". Didn't we always maintain, they say, that the bourgeois-democratic revolution is completed only by the "revolutionary-democratic dictatorship of the proletariat and the peasantry"? Is the agrarian revolution, which is also a bourgeois-democratic revolution, completed? Is it not a fact, on the contrary, that it has *not even* started?

My answer is: The Bolshevik slogans and ideas *on the whole* have been confirmed by history; but *concretely* things have worked out *differently;* they are more original, more peculiar, more varied than anyone could have expected.

To ignore or overlook this fact would mean taking after those "old Bolsheviks" who more than once already have played so regrettable a role in the history of our Party by reiterating formulas senselessly *learned by rote* instead of *studying* the specific features of the new and living reality.

'The revolutionary-democratic dictatorship of the proletariat and the peasantry" has *already* become a reality[10] in the Russian revolution, for this "formula" envisages only a *relation of classes*, and not a *concrete political institution implementing* this relation, this co-operation. "The Soviet of Workers' and Soldiers' Deputies"— there you have the "revolutionary-democratic dictatorship of the proletariat and the peasantry" already accomplished in reality.

This formula is already antiquated. Events have moved it from tile realm of formulas into the realm of reality, clothed it with flesh and bone, concretised it and *thereby* modified it.

A new and different task now faces us: to effect a split *within* this dictatorship between the proletarian elements (the anti-defencist, internationalist, "Communist" elements, who stand for a transition to the commune) and the *small-proprietor* or *petty-bourgeois* elements (Chkheidze, Tsereteli, Steklov, the Socialist-Revolutionaries and the other revolutionary defencists, who are opposed to moving towards the commune and are in favour of "supporting" the bourgeoisie and the bourgeois government).

The person who *now* speaks only of a "revolutionary democratic dictatorship of the proletariat and the peasantry" is behind the times, consequently, he has in effect *gone over* to the petty bourgeoisie against the proletarian class struggle; that person should be consigned to the archive of "Bolshevik" pre-revolutionary antiques (it may be called the archive of "old Bolsheviks").

---

[10] In a certain form and to a certain extent. —*Lenin*

The revolutionary-democratic dictatorship of the proletariat and the peasantry has already been realised, but in a highly original manner, and with a number of extremely important modifications. I shall deal with them separately in one of my next letters. For the present, it is essential to grasp the incontestable truth that a Marxist must take cognisance of real life, of the true facts of *reality,* and not cling to a theory of yesterday, which, like all theories, at best only outlines the main and the general, only *comes near* to embracing life in all its complexity.

"Theory, my friend, is grey, but green is the eternal tree of life."[11]

To deal with the question of "completion" of the bourgeois revolution *in the old way* is to sacrifice living Marxism to the dead letter.

According to the old way of thinking, the rule of the bourgeoisie could and should be *followed* by the rule of the proletariat and the peasantry, by their dictatorship.

In real life, however, things have *already* turned out *differently;* there has been an extremely original, novel and unprecedented *interlacing of the one with the other.* We have side by side, existing together, simultaneously, *both* the rule of the bourgeoisie (the government of Lvov and Guchkov) and a revolutionary-democratic dictatorship of the proletariat and the peasantry, which is *voluntarily* ceding power to the bourgeoisie, voluntarily making itself an appendage of the bourgeoisie.

For it must not be forgotten that actually, in Petrograd, the power is in the hands of the workers and soldiers; the new government is *not* using and cannot use violence against them, because *there is no* police, *no* army standing apart from the people, *no* officialdom standing all-powerful *above* the people. This is a fact, the kind of fact that is characteristic of a state of the Paris Commune type. This fact does not fit into the old schemes. One must know how to adapt schemes to facts, instead of reiterating the now meaningless words about a "dictatorship of the proletariat and the peasantry" *in general.*

To throw more light on this question let us approach it from another angle.

A Marxist must not abandon the ground of careful analysis of class relations. The bourgeoisie is in power. But is not the mass of the peasants *also* a bourgeoisie, only of a different social stratum, of

---

[11] Lenin here quotes the words of Mephistopheles from Goethe's tragedy *Faust.* Erster Teil, Studierzimmer.

a different kind, of a different character? Whence does it follow that *this* stratum *cannot* come to power, thus "completing" the bourgeois-democratic revolution? Why should this be impossible?

This is how the old Bolsheviks often argue.

My reply is that it is quite possible. But, in assessing a given situation, a Marxist must proceed *not* from what is possible, but from what is real.

And the reality reveals the *fact* that freely elected soldiers' and peasants' deputies are freely joining the second, parallel government, and are freely supplementing, developing and completing it. And, just as freely, they are *surrendering* power to the bourgeoisie—a fact which does not in the least contravene the theory of Marxism, for we have always known and repeatedly pointed out that the bourgeoisie maintains itself in power *not* only by force but, also by virtue of the lack of class-consciousness and organisation, the routinism and downtrodden state of the masses.

In view of this present-day reality, it is simply ridiculous to turn one's back on the fact and talk about "possibilities".

Possibly the peasantry may seize all the land and all the power. Far from forgetting this possibility, far from confining myself to the present, I definitely and clearly formulate the agrarian programme, taking into account the *new* phenomenon, i.e., the deeper cleavage between the agricultural labourers and the poor peasants on the one hand, and the peasant proprietors on the other.

But there is also another possibility; it is possible that the peasants will take the advice of the petty-bourgeois party of the Socialist-Revolutionaries, which has yielded to the influence of the bourgeoisie, has adopted a defencist stand, and which advises waiting for the Constituent Assembly, although not even the date of its convocation has yet been fixed.[12]

It is possible that the peasants will *maintain* and prolong their deal with the bourgeoisie, a deal which they have now concluded through the Soviets of Workers' and Soldiers' Deputies not only in form, but in fact.

Many things are possible. It would be a great mistake to forget the agrarian movement and the agrarian programme. But it would

---

[12] Lest my words be misinterpreted, I shall say at once that I am positively in favour of the *Soviets* of Agricultural Labourers and Peasants *immediately* taking over *all* the land; but they should *thesleves* observe the strictest order and discipline, not permit the slightest dam age to machines, structures, or livestock, and in no case disorganise agriculture and grain production, but rather *develop* them, for the soldiers need *twice* as much bread, and the people must not be allowed to starve. —*Lenin*

be no less a mistake to forget the *reality,* which reveals the fact that an *agreement,* or—to use a more exact, less legal, but more class-economic term—*class collaboration* exists between the bourgeoisie and the peasantry.

When this fact ceases to be a fact, when the peasantry separates from the bourgeoisie, seizes the land and power despite the bourgeoisie, that will be a new stage in the bourgeois-democratic revolution; and that matter will be dealt with separately.

A Marxist who, in view of the possibility of such a future stage, was to forget his duties in *the present,* when the peasantry is *in agreement* with the bourgeoisie, would turn petty bourgeois. For he would in practice be preaching to the proletariat *confidence* in the petty bourgeoisie ("this petty bourgeoisie, this peasantry, must separate from the bourgeoisie while the bourgeois-democratic revolution is still on"). Because of the "possibility" of so pleasing and sweet a future, in which the peasantry would *not* be the tail of the bourgeoisie, in which the Socialist-Revolutionaries, the Chkheidzes, Tseretelis, and Steklovs would *not* be an appendage of the bourgeois government—because of the "possibility" of so pleasing a future, he would be forgetting *the unpleasant present,* in which the peasantry still forms the tail of the bourgeoisie, and in which the Socialist-Revolutionaries and Social-Democrats have not yet given up their role as an appendage of the bourgeois government, as "His Majesty" Lvov's Opposition.[13]

This hypothetical person would resemble a sweetish Louis Blanc, or a sugary Kautskyite, but certainly not a revolutionary Marxist.

But are we not in danger of falling into subjectivism, of wanting to arrive at the socialist revolution by "skipping" the bourgeois-democratic revolution—which is not yet completed and has not yet exhausted the peasant movement?

I might be incurring this danger if I said: "No Tsar, but a *workers'* government." But I did *not* say that, I said something else. I said that there *can be no* government (barring a bourgeois government) in Russia *other than* that of the Soviets of Workers', Agricultural Labourers', Soldiers', and Peasants' Deputies. I said that power in Russia now can pass from Guchkov and Lvov *only* to

---

[13] The expression "His Majesty's Opposition" belongs to P. N. Milyukov, the leader of the Cadet Party. In a speech made at a luncheon given by the Lord Mayor of London on June 19 (July 2), 1909, Milyukov said: "So long as there is a legislative chamber in Russia which controls the budget, the Russian Opposition will remain the Opposition of His Majesty, not to His Majesty" (Flerh No. 167, June 21 [July 4]. 1909).

these Soviets. And in these Soviets, as it happens, it is the peasants, the soldiers, i.e., petty bourgeoisie, who preponderate, to use a scientific, Marxist term, a class characterisation, and not a common, man-in-the-street, professional characterisation.

In my theses, I absolutely ensured myself against skipping over the peasant movement, which has not outlived itself, or the petty-bourgeois movement in general, against any *playing* at "seizure of power" by a workers' government, against any kind of Blanquist adventurism; for I pointedly referred to the experience of the Paris Commune. And this experience, as we know, and as Marx proved at length in 1871 and Engels in 1891,[14] absolutely excludes Blanquism, absolutely ensures the direct, immediate and unquestionable rule of the *majority* and the activity of the masses only to the extent that the majority itself acts *consciously.*

In the theses, I very definitely reduced the question to one of *a struggle for influence within* the Soviets of Workers', Agricultural Labourers', Peasants', and Soldiers' Deputies. To leave no shadow of doubt on this score, I *twice* emphasised in the theses the need for patient and persistent "explanatory" work "adapted to the *practical* needs of the *masses*".

Ignorant persons or renegades from Marxism, like Mr. Plekhanov, may shout about anarchism, Blanquism, and so forth. But those who want to think and learn cannot fail to understand that Blanquism means the seizure of power by a minority, whereas the Soviets are *admittedly* the direct and immediate organisation of the *majority* of the people. Work confined to a struggle for influence *within* these Soviets cannot, simply *cannot,* stray into the swamp of Blanquism. Nor can it stray into the swamp of anarchism, for anarchism denies *the need for a state and state power* in the period of *transition* from the rule of the bourgeoisie to the rule of the proletariat, whereas I, with a precision that precludes any possibility of misinterpretation, *advocate* the need for a state in this period, although, in accordance with Marx and the lessons of the Paris Commune, I advocate not the usual parliamentary bourgeois state, but a state *without* a standing army, *without* a police opposed to the people, *without* an officialdom placed above the people.

When Mr. Plekhanov, in his newspaper *Yedinstvo,* shouts with all his might that this is anarchism, he is merely giving further proof of his break with Marxism. Challenged by me in Pravda (No. 26) to tell us what Marx and Engels taught on the subject in 1871, 1872 and 1875,[6] Mr. Plekhanov can only preserve silence on the question at issue and shout out abuse after the manner of the enraged bourgeoisie.

Mr. Plekhanov, the ex-Marxist, has *absolutely* failed to understand the Marxist doctrine of the state. Incidentally, the germs of this lack of understanding are also to he found in his German pamphlet on anarchism.

Now let us see how Comrade Y. Kamenev, in *Pravda* No. 27, formulates his "disagreements" with my theses and with the views expressed above. This will help us to grasp them more clearly.

"As for Comrade Lenin's general scheme," writes Comrade Kamenev, "it appears to us unacceptable, inasmuch as it proceeds from the assumption that the bourgeois-democratic revolution is *completed,* and builds on the immediate transformation of this revolution into a socialist revolution.'

There are two big mistakes here.

First. The question of "completion" of the bourgeois-democratic revolution is *stated* wrongly. The question is put in an abstract, simple, so to speak one-colour, way, which does *not* correspond to the objective reality. To put the question *this way,* to ask *now* "whether the bourgeois-democratic revolution is completed" and say *no more,* is to prevent oneself from seeing the exceedingly complex reality, which, is at least two-coloured. This is in theory. In practice, it means surrendering helplessly to *petty-bourgeois revolutionism.*

Indeed, reality shows us *both* the passing of power into the hands of the bourgeoisie (a "completed" bourgeois-democratic revolution of the usual type) and, side by side with the real government, the existence of a parallel government which represents the "revolutionary-democratic dictatorship of the proletariat and the peasantry". This "second government" has *itself* ceded the power to the bourgeoisie, has chained *itself* to the bourgeois government.

Is this reality covered by Comrade Kamenev's old-Bolshevik formula, which says that "the bourgeois-democratic revolution is not completed"?

It is not. The formula is obsolete. It is no good at all. It is dead. And it is no use trying to revive it.

Second. A practical question. Who knows whether it is still possible at present for a special "revolutionary-democratic dictatorship of the proletariat and the peasantry", *detached* from the bourgeois government, to emerge in Russia? Marxist tactics cannot be based on the unknown.

But *if* this is still possible, then there is one, and only one, way towards it, namely, an immediate, resolute, and irrevocable separation of the proletarian Communist elements from the petty-bourgeois elements.

Why?

Because the entire petty bourgeoisie has, not by chance but of necessity, turned towards chauvinism (=defencism), towards "support" of the bourgeoisie, towards dependence on it, towards the *fear* of having to do without it, etc., etc.

How can the petty bourgeoisie be "pushed" into power, if even now it can take the power, but *does not want to?*

This can be done only by separating the proletarian, the Communist, party, by waging a proletarian class struggle *free from* the timidity of those petty bourgeois. Only the consolidation of the proletarians who are free from the influence of the petty bourgeoisie in deed and not only in word can make the ground so hot under the feet of the petty bourgeoisie that it will be *obliged* under certain circumstances to take the power; it is even within the bounds of possibility that Guchkov and Milyukov—again under certain circumstances—will be forgiving full and sole power to Chkheidze, Tsereteli, the S.R.s, and Steklov, since, after all, these are *"defencists".*

To separate the proletarian elements of the Soviets (i.e., the proletarian, Communist, party) from the petty-bourgeois elements right now, immediately and irrevocably, is to give correct expression to the interests of the movement in *either* of two possible events: in the event that Russia will yet experience a special "dictatorship of the proletariat and the peasantry" independent of the bourgeoisie, and in the event that the petty bourgeoisie will not be able to tear itself away from the bourgeoisie and will oscillate eternally (that is, until socialism is established) between us and it.

To be guided in one's activities merely by the simple formula, "the bourgeois-democratic revolution is not completed", is like taking it upon oneself to guarantee that the petty bourgeoisie is definitely capable of being independent of the bourgeoisie. To do so is to throw oneself at the given moment on the mercy of the petty bourgeoisie.

Incidentally, in connection with the "formula" of the dictatorship of the proletariat and the peasantry, it is worth mentioning that, in *Two Tactics* (July 1905), I made a point of emphasising *(Twelve Years,* p. 435) this:

"Like everything else in the world, the revolutionary-democratic dictatorship of the proletariat and the peasantry has a past and a future. Its past is autocracy, serfdom, monarchy, and privilege....Its future is the struggle against private property, the struggle of the wage-worker against the employer, the struggle for socialism...."

Comrade Kamenev's mistake is that even in 1917 he sees only *the past* of the revolutionary-democratic dictatorship of the proletariat and the peasantry. As a matter of fact its *future* has already begun, for the interests and policies of the wage-worker and the petty proprietor have *actually* diverged already, even in such an important question as that of "defencism", that of the attitude towards the imperialist war.

This brings me to the second mistake in Comrade Kamenev's argument quoted above. He criticises me, saying that my scheme "builds" on "the immediate transformation of this {bourgeois-democratic} revolution into a socialist revolution".

This is incorrect. I not only do not "build" on the "immediate transformation" of our revolution into a *socialist* one, but I actually warn against it, when in Thesis No. 8, I state: "It is *not* our *immediate* task to 'introduce' socialism...".

Is it not clear that no person who builds on the immediate transformation of our revolution into a socialist revolution could be opposed to the immediate task of introducing socialism?

Moreover, even a "commune state" (i.e., a state organised along the lines of the Paris Commune) *cannot* be introduced in Russia "immediately", because to do that it would be necessary for the *majority* of the deputies in all (or in most) Soviets to clearly recognise all the erroneousness and harm of the tactics and policy pursued by the S.R.s, Chkheidze, Tsereteli, Steklov, etc. As for me, I declared unmistakably that in this respect I "build" only on "patient" explaining (does one have to be patient to bring about a change which can be effected "immediately"?).

Comrade Kamenev has somewhat overreached himself in his eagerness, and has repeated the bourgeois prejudice about the Paris Commune having wanted to introduce socialism "immediately". This is not so. The Commune, unfortunately, was too slow in introducing socialism. The real essence of the Commune is not where the bourgeois usually looks for it, but in the creation of a *state* of a special type. Such a state has *already* arisen in Russia, it is the Soviets of Workers' and Soldiers' Deputies!

Comrade Kamenev has not pondered on the *fact*, the significance, of the *existing* Soviets, their identity, in point of type and socio-political character, with the commune state, and instead of studying the *fact,* he began to talk about something I was supposed to be "building" on for the "immediate" future. The result is, unfortunately, a repetition of the method used by many bourgeois: from the question as to *what are* the Soviets, whether they are of a *higher* type than a parliamentary republic, whether they are *more useful* for the people, *more democratic, more convenient* for the struggle, for combating, for instance, the grain shortage, etc.—from this real, urgent, vital issue, attention is diverted to the empty, would-be scientific, but actually hollow, professorially dead question of "building on an immediate transformation".

An idle question falsely presented. I "build" *only* on this, *exclusively* on this—that the workers, soldiers and peasants will deal better than the officials, better than the police, with the difficult *practical,* problems of producing more grain, distributing it better and keeping the soldiers better supplied, etc., etc.

I am deeply convinced that the Soviets will make the independent activity of the *masses* a reality more quickly and effectively than will a parliamentary republic (I shall compare the two types of states in greater detail in another letter). They will more effectively, more practically and more correctly decide what *steps* can be taken towards socialism and how these steps should be taken. Control over a bank, the merging of all banks into one, is *not yet* socialism, but it is *a step towards* socialism. Today such steps are being taken in Germany by the Junkers and the bourgeoisie against the people. Tomorrow the Soviet will be able to take these steps more effectively for the benefit of the people if the whole state power is in its hands.

What *compels* such steps?

Famine. Economic disorganisation. Imminent collapse. The horrors of war. The horrors of the wounds inflicted on mankind by the war.

Comrade Kamenev concludes his article with the remark that "in a broad discussion he hopes to carry his point of view, which is the only possible one for revolutionary Social-Democracy if it wishes to and should remain to the very end the party of the revolutionary masses of the proletariat and not turn into a group of Communist propagandists".

It seems to me that these words betray a completely erroneous estimate of the situation. Comrade Kamenev contraposes to a "party of the masses" a "group of propagandists". But the "masses" have now succumbed to the craze of "revolutionary" defencism. Is it not more becoming for internationalists at this moment to show that they can resist "mass" intoxication rather than to "wish to remain" with the masses, i.e., to succumb to the general epidemic? Have we not seen how in all the belligerent countries of Europe the chauvinists tried to justify themselves on the grounds that they wished to "remain with the masses"? Must we not be able to remain for a time in the minority against the "mass" intoxication? Is it not the work of the propagandists at the present moment that forms the key point for *disentangling* the proletarian line from the defencist and petty-bourgeois "mass" intoxication? It was this fusion of the masses, proletarian and non-proletarian, regardless of class differences within the masses, that formed one of the conditions for the defencist epidemic. To speak contemptuously of a "group of propagandists" advocating a *proletarian* line does not seem to be very becoming.

Introduction to "The Character of the Russian Revolution: Three Concepts"

The Permanent Revolution was presented first by Marx and Engels in the Communist Manifesto during the revolutionary situation of 1848. It was stated as a long-term strategy in their first Address to the Communist League two years later. Lenin applied it to the Russian condition in April 1917. Trotsky had projected its outlines before the previous, abortive rising of 1905. This pamphlet provides a concise explanation of what it is.

Fundamentally, it remarks that there can be only two forms of revolutionary seizure of state power: that of the urban bourgeoisie and that of the proletariat. Perception of this is blurred too often by the fact that in most countries of the world the majority of the population is composed of rural capitalists, often small capitalists, the peasants. On the one hand their role is crucial; they can decide which urban class gives its stamp to the victorious revolutionary state. On the other, they cannot give their own distinct stamp to it. A peasant state will be a bourgeois state, operated by and for urban capital. However, the workers have to compromise their maximum programme (which they cannot achieve on a national basis, anyway) to allow for the rural capitalist aspirations of the peasant majority. The result will be a workers state, that will constitute a transitional form of society between capitalism and world socialism.

There are two diversions from this strategy. One is that promoted by Stalin after Lenin's death: one of holding back the social change to provide a capitalist regime, in town and country, although one formally more enlightened than the average bourgeois order. This has opened graves for many revolutions in the last century. Moreover, although some have been said to have been won by its operation, detailed investigation shows that their leaderships have gone beyond the straitjacket of completing the bourgeois revolution before that of the workers. The alternative danger is that of trying to do without the peasantry. This has been easy in the advanced capitalist countries, where capital has decimated the rural interest. In practice, it means not just abandoning the immediate concessions to small rural capital, but abandoning the struggle for the democratic rights that were identified initially with the bourgeois seizure of state power. In Ireland, this has been used as an excuse for accepting as final the continuing partition of the country. That this has been even less successful than the Stalinite deviation has been used, inevitably, by the Stalinites as a smear on the actual process and strategy of Permanent Revolution.

For this reason, it is worthwhile publishing this explanation

Trotsky wrote it as a chapter in his unfinished life of Lenin. After his death, it became an appendix to his more nearly completed life of his opponent, Stalin.

Leon Trotsky: "The Character of the Russian Revolution: Three Concepts"

The revolution of 1905 became not only "the dress rehearsal of 1917" but also the laboratory from which emerged all the basic groupings of Russian political thought and where all tendencies and shadings within Russian Marxism took shape or were outlined.

The centre of the disputes and differences was naturally occupied by the question of the historical character of the Russian revolution and its future paths of development. In and of itself this war of conceptions and prognoses does not relate directly to the biography of Stalin, who took no independent part in it. Those few propaganda articles which he wrote on the subject are without the slightest theoretical interest. Scores of Bolsheviks, with pens in hand, popularized the very same ideas and did it much more ably.

A critical exposition of the revolutionary conception of Bolshevism should, in the very nature of things, have entered into a biography of Lenin. However, theories have a fate of their own.

If in the period of the first revolution and thereafter up to 1923, when revolutionary doctrines were elaborated and realized, Stalin held no independent position then, from 1924 on, the situation changes abruptly. There opens up the epoch of bureaucratic reaction and of drastic reviews of the past. The film of the revolution is run off in reverse. Old doctrines are submitted to new appraisals or new interpretations. Quite unexpectedly, at first sight, the centre of attention is held by the conception of "the permanent revolution" as the fountainhead of all the blunderings of "Trotskyism."

For a number of years thereafter, the criticism of this conception constitutes the main content of the theoretical – *sit venio verbo* – work of Stalin and his collaborators. It may be said that the whole of Stalinism, taken on the theoretical plane, grew out of the criticism of the theory of the permanent revolution as it was formulated in 1905.

To this extent the exposition of this theory, as distinct from the theories of the Mensheviks and Bolsheviks, cannot fail to enter into this book[14], even if in the form of an appendix.

---

[14] First written for publication in a biography of Lenin, upon which Trotsky worked in the last years of his life, this was rewritten for publication in his biography of Stalin.

Russia's Combined Development

The development of Russia is characterized first of all by backwardness. Historical backwardness does not, however, signify a simple reproduction of the development of advanced countries, with merely a delay of one or two centuries. It engenders an entirely new "combined" social formation in which the latest conquests of capitalist technique and structure root themselves into relations of feudal and pre-feudal barbarism, transforming and subjecting them and creating a peculiar interrelationship of classes.

The same thing applies in the sphere of ideas. Precisely because of her historical tardiness, Russia turned out to be the only European country where Marxism as a doctrine and the Social Democracy as a party attained powerful development even before the bourgeois revolution. It is only natural that the problem of the correlation between the struggle for democracy and the struggle for socialism was submitted to the most profound theoretical analysis precisely in Russia.

Idealist-democrats, chiefly the Narodniks, refused superstitiously to recognize the impending revolution as bourgeois. They labelled it "democratic" seeking by means of a neutral political formula to mask its social content – not only from others but also from themselves. But in the struggle against Narodnikism, Plekhanov, the founder of Russian Marxism, established as long ago as the early eighties of the last century that Russia had no reason whatever to expect a privileged path of development, that like other "profane" nations, she would have to pass through the purgatory of capitalism and that precisely along this path she would acquire political freedom indispensable for the further struggle of the proletariat for socialism.

Plekhanov not only separated the bourgeois revolution as a task from the socialist revolution – which he postponed to the indefinite future – but he depicted for each of these entirely different combinations of forces. Political freedom was to be achieved by the proletariat in alliance with the liberal bourgeoisie; after many decades and on a higher level of capitalist development, the proletariat would then carry out the socialist revolution in direct struggle against the bourgeoisie.

"To the Russian intellectual it always seems that to recognize our revolution as bourgeois is to discolour it, degrade it, debase it ... For the proletariat the struggle for political freedom and for the democratic republic in bourgeois society is simply a necessary stage in the struggle for the socialist revolution."

"Marxists are absolutely convinced," he wrote in 1905, "of the bourgeois character of the Russian revolution. What does this mean? This means that those democratic transformations which have become indispensable for Russia do not, in and of themselves, signify the undermining of capitalism, the undermining of bourgeois rule, but on the contrary they clear the soil, for the first time and in a real way, for a broad and swift, for a European and not an Asiatic development of capitalism. They will make possible for the first time the rule of the bourgeoisie as a class ...

"We cannot leap over the bourgeois democratic framework of the Russian revolution," he insisted, "but we can extend this framework to a colossal degree."

That is to say, we can create within bourgeois society much more favourable conditions for the future struggle of the proletariat. Within these limits Lenin followed Plekhanov. The bourgeois character of the revolution served both factions of the Russian Social Democracy as their starting point.

It is quite natural that under these conditions, Koba (Stalin) did not go in his propaganda beyond those popular formulas which constitute the common property of Bolsheviks as well as Mensheviks.

"The Constituent Assembly," he wrote in January 1905, "elected on the basis of equal, direct and secret universal suffrage-this is what we must now fight for! Only this Assembly will give us the democratic republic, so urgently needed by us for our struggle for socialism."

The bourgeois republic as an arena for a protracted class struggle for the socialist goal such is the perspective.

In 1907, i.e., after innumerable discussions in the press both in Petersburg and abroad and after a serious testing of theoretical prognoses in the experiences of the first revolution, Stalin wrote:

"That our revolution is bourgeois, that it must conclude by destroying the feudal and not the capitalist order, that it can be crowned only by the democratic republic – on this, it seems, all are agreed in our party."

Stalin spoke not of what the revolution begins with, but of what it ends with, and he limited it in advance and quite categorically to "only the democratic republic." We would seek in vain in his writings for even a hint of any perspective of a socialist revolution in connection with a democratic overturn. This remained his position even at the beginning of the February revolution in 1917 up to Lenin's arrival in Petersburg.

The Menshevik View

For Plekhanov, Axelrod and the leaders of Menshevism in general, the sociological characterization of the revolution as bourgeois was valuable politically above all because in advance it prohibited provoking the bourgeoisie by the spectre of socialism and "repelling" it into the camp of reaction.

"The social relations of Russia have ripened only for the bourgeois revolution," said the chief tactician of Menshevism, Axelrod, at the Unity Congress. "In the face of the universal deprivation of political rights in our country there cannot even be talk of a direct battle between the proletariat and other classes for political power ... The proletariat is fighting for conditions of bourgeois development. The objective historical conditions make it the destiny of our proletariat to inescapably collaborate with the bourgeoisie in the struggle against the common enemy." The content of the Russian revolution was therewith limited in advance to those transformations which are compatible with the interests and views of the liberal bourgeoisie.

It is precisely at this point that the basic disagreement between the two factions begins.

Bolshevism absolutely refused to recognize that the Russian bourgeoisie was capable of leading its own revolution to the end. With infinitely greater power and consistency than Plekhanov, Lenin advanced the agrarian question as the central problem of the democratic overturn in Russia. "The crux of the Russian revolution," he repeated, "is the agrarian (land) question. Conclusions concerning the defeat or victory of the revolution must be based ... on the calculation of the condition of the masses in the struggle for land."

Together with Plekhanov, Lenin viewed the peasantry as a petty-bourgeois class; the peasant land program as a program of bourgeois progress. "Nationalization is a bourgeois measure," he insisted at the Unity Congress. "It will give an impulse to the development of capitalism; it will sharpen the class struggle, strengthen the mobilization of the land, cause an influx of capital into agriculture, lower the price of grain." Notwithstanding the indubitable bourgeois character of the agrarian revolution the Russian bourgeoisie remains, however, hostile to the expropriation of landed estates and precisely for this reason strives toward a compromise with the monarchy on the basis of a constitution on the Prussian pattern. To Plekhanov's idea of an alliance between the proletariat and the liberal bourgeoisie Lenin counterposed the idea of an alliance between the proletariat and the peasantry. The task of the revolutionary collaboration of these two classes he proclaimed to be the establishment of a "democratic dictatorship," as the only means of radically cleansing Russia of feudal rubbish, of creating a free farmers' system and clearing the road for the development of capitalism along American and not Prussian lines.

The victory of the revolution, he wrote, can be crowned "only by a dictatorship because the accomplishment of transformations immediately and urgently needed by the proletariat and the peasantry will evoke the desperate resistance of the landlords, the big bourgeoisie and Czarism. Without the dictatorship it will be impossible to break the resistance, and repel the counter-revolutionary attempts. But this will of course be not a socialist but a democratic dictatorship. It will not be able to touch (without a whole series of transitional stages of revolutionary development) the foundations of capitalism. It will be able, in the best case, to realize a radical redivision of landed property in favour of the peasantry, introduce a consistent and full democratism up to instituting the republic, root out all Asiatic and feudal features not only from the day-to-day life of the village but also of the factory, put a beginning to a serious improvement of workers' conditions and raise their living standards and, last but not least, carry over the revolutionary conflagration to Europe."

Vulnerability of Lenin's Position

Lenin's conception represented an enormous step forward insofar as it proceeded not from constitutional reforms but from the agrarian overturn as the central task of the revolution and singled out the only realistic combination of social forces for its accomplishment.

The weak point of Lenin's conception, however, was the internally contradictory idea of "the democratic dictatorship of the proletariat and the peasantry." Lenin himself underscored the fundamental limitation of this "dictatorship" when he openly called it *bourgeois*. By this he meant to say that for the sake of preserving its alliance with the peasantry the proletariat would in the coming revolution have to forego the direct posing of the socialist tasks. But this would signify the renunciation by the proletariat of its own dictatorship. Consequently, the gist of the matter involved the dictatorship of the peasantry even if with the participation of the workers.

On certain occasions Lenin said just this. For example, at the Stockholm Conference, in refuting Plekhanov who came out against the "utopia" of the seizure of power, Lenin said: "What program is under discussion? The agrarian. Who is assumed to seize power under this, program? The revolutionary peasantry. Is Lenin mixing up the power of the proletariat with this peasantry?" No, he says referring to himself: Lenin sharply differentiates the socialist power of the proletariat from the bourgeois democratic power of the peasantry. "But how," he exclaims again, "is a victorious peasant revolution possible without the seizure of power by the revolutionary peasantry?" In this polemical formula Lenin reveals with special clarity the vulnerability of his position.

The peasantry is dispersed over the surface of an enormous country whose key junctions are the cities. The peasantry itself is incapable of even formulating its own interests inasmuch as in each district these appear differently. The economic link between the provinces is created by the market and the railways but both the market and the railways are in the hands of the cities. In seeking to tear itself away from the restrictions of the village and to generalize its own interests, the peasantry inescapably falls into political dependence upon the city. Finally, the peasantry is heterogeneous in its social relations as well: the kulak stratum naturally seeks to swing it to an alliance with the urban bourgeoisie while the other strata of the village pull to the side of the urban workers. Under these conditions the peasantry as such is completely incapable of conquering power.

True enough, in ancient China, revolutions placed the peasantry in power or, more precisely, placed the military leaders of peasant uprisings in power. This led each time to a redivision of the land and the establishment of a new "peasant" dynasty, whereupon history would begin from the beginning; with a new concentration of usury, and a new uprising.

So long as the revolution preserves its purely peasant character society is incapable of emerging from these hopeless and vicious circles. This was the basis of ancient Asiatic history, including ancient Russian history. In Europe beginning with the close of the Middle Ages each victorious peasant uprising placed in power not a peasant government but a left urban party. To put it more precisely, a peasant uprising turned out victorious exactly to the degree to which it succeeded in strengthening the position of the revolutionary section of the urban population. In bourgeois Russia of the twentieth century these could not even be talk of the seizure of power by the revolutionary peasantry.

Attitude toward Liberalism

The attitude toward the liberal bourgeoisie was, as has been said, the touchstone of the differentiation between revolutionists and opportunists in the ranks of the social democrats. How far could the Russian revolution go? What would be the character of the future revolutionary Provisional Government? What tasks would confront it? And in what order? These questions with all their importance could be correctly posed only on the basis of the fundamental character of the policy of the proletariat, and the character of this policy was in turn determined first of all by the attitude toward the liberal bourgeoisie. Plekhanov obviously and stubbornly shut his eyes to the fundamental conclusion of the political history of the 19th century: Whenever the proletariat comes forward as an independent force the bourgeoisie shifts over to the camp of the counter-revolution. The more audacious the mass struggle all the swifter is the reactionary degeneration of liberalism. No one has yet invented a means for paralyzing the effects of the law of the class struggle.

"We must cherish the support of non-proletarian parties," repeated Plekhanov during the years of the first revolution, "and not repel them from us by tactless actions." By monotonous preachments of this sort, the philosopher of Marxism indicated that the living dynamics of society was unattainable to him. "Tactlessness" can repel an individual sensitive intellectual. Classes and parties are attracted or repelled by social interests. "It can be stated with certainty," replied Lenin to Plekhanov, "that the liberals and landlords will forgive you millions of 'tactless acts' but will not forgive you a summons to take away the land." And not only the landlords. The tops of the bourgeoisie are bound up with the landowners by the unity of property interests, and more narrowly by the system of banks. The tops of the petty bourgeoisie and the intelligentsia are materially and morally dependent upon the big and middle proprietors-they are all afraid of the independent mass movement. Meanwhile, in order to overthrow Czarism, it was necessary to rouse tens upon tens of millions of oppressed to a heroic, self-renouncing, unfettered revolutionary assault that would halt at nothing. The masses can rise to an insurrection only under the banner of their own interests and consequently in the spirit of irreconcilable hostility toward the exploiting classes beginning with the landlords. The "repulsion" of the oppositional bourgeoisie away from the revolutionary workers and peasants was therefore the immanent law of the revolution itself and could not be avoided by means of diplomacy or "tact."

Each additional month confirmed the Leninist appraisal of liberalism. Contrary to the best hopes of the Mensheviks, the Cadets not only did not prepare to take their place at the head of the "bourgeois" revolution but on the contrary they found their historical mission more and more in the struggle against it.

After the crushing of the December uprising the liberals, who occupied the political limelight thanks to the ephemeral Duma, sought with all their might to justify themselves before the monarchy and explain away their insufficiently active counter-revolutionary conduct in the autumn of 1905 when danger threatened the most sacred props of "culture." The leader of the liberals, Miliukov, who conducted the behind-the-scenes negotiations with the Winter Palace, quite correctly proved in the press that at the end of 1905 the Cadets could not even show themselves before the masses. "Those who now chide the (Cadet) party," he wrote, "because it did not protest at the time by arranging meetings against the revolutionary illusions of Trotskyism ... simply do not understand or do not remember the moods prevailing at the time among the democratic public gatherings at meetings." By the "illusions of Trotskyism" the liberal leader understood the independent policy of the proletariat which attracted to the soviets the sympathies of the nethermost layers in the cities, of the soldiers, peasants, and all the oppressed, and which owing to this repelled the "educated society." The evolution of the Mensheviks unfolded along parallel lines. They had to justify themselves more and more frequently before the liberals, because they had turned out in a bloc with Trotsky after October 1905. The explanations of Martov, the talented publicist of the Mensheviks, came down to this, that it was necessary to make concessions to the "revolutionary illusions" of the masses.

Stalin's Part in the Dispute

In Tiflis the political groupings took shape on the same principled basis as in Petersburg. "To smash reaction," wrote the leader of the Caucasian Mensheviks, Zhordanya, "to conquer and carry, through the Constitution – this will depend upon the conscious unification and the striving for a single goal on the part of the forces of the proletariat and the bourgeoisie ... It is true that the peasantry will be drawn into the movement, investing it with an elemental character, but the decisive role will nevertheless be played by these two classes while the peasant movement will add grist to their mill." Lenin mocked at the fears of Zhordanya that an irreconcilable policy toward the bourgeoisie would doom the workers to impotence. Zhordanya "discusses the question of the possible isolation of the proletariat in a democratic overturn and forgets ... about the peasantry! Of all the possible allies of the proletariat he knows and is enamoured of the landlord-liberals. And he does not know the peasants. And this in the Caucasus!" The refutations of Lenin while correct in essence simplify the problem on one point. Zhordanya did not "forget" about the peasantry and, as may be gathered from the hint of Lenin himself, could not have possibly forgotten about it in the Caucasus where the peasantry was stormily rising at the time under the banner of the Mensheviks. Zhordanya saw in the peasantry, however, not so much a political ally as a historical battering ram which could and should be utilized by the bourgeoisie in alliance with the proletariat. He did not believe that the peasantry was capable of becoming a leading or even an independent force in the revolution and in this he was not wrong; but he also did not believe that the proletariat was capable of leading the peasant uprising to victory – and in this was his fatal mistake. The Menshevik idea of the alliance of the proletariat with the bourgeoisie actually signified the subjection to the liberals of both the workers and the peasants. The reactionary utopianism of this program was determined by the fact that the far advanced dismemberment of the classes paralyzed the bourgeoisie in advance as a revolutionary factor. In this fundamental question the right was wholly on the side of Bolshevism: the chase after an alliance with the liberal bourgeoisie would inescapably counterpose the Social Democracy to the revolutionary movement of workers and peasants. In 1905 the Mensheviks still lacked courage to draw all the necessary conclusions from their theory of the "bourgeois" revolution. In 1917 they drew their ideas to their logical conclusion and broke their heads.

On the question of the attitude to the liberals, Stalin stood during the years of the first revolution on Lenin's side. It must be stated that during this period even the majority of the rank-and-file Mensheviks were closer to Lenin than to Plekhanov on issues touching the oppositional bourgeoisie. A contemptuous attitude to the liberals was the literary tradition of intellectual radicalism. One would however labour in vain to seek from Koba an independent contribution on this question, an analysis of the Caucasian social relations, new arguments or even a new formulation of old arguments. The leader of the Caucasian Mensheviks, Zhordanya, was far more independent in relation to Plekhanov than Stalin was in relation to Lenin. "In vain the Messrs. Liberals seek," wrote Koba after January 9, "to save the tottering throne of the Czar. In vain are they extending to the Czar the hand of assistance!

"The aroused popular masses are preparing for the revolution and not for reconciliation with the Czar ... Yes, gentlemen, in vain are your efforts. The Russian revolution is inevitable and it is as inevitable as the inevitable rising of the sun! Can you stop the rising sun? That is the question!" And so forth and so on. Higher than this Koba did not rise. Two and a half years later, in repeating Lenin almost literally, he wrote: "The Russian liberal bourgeoisie is anti-revolutionary. It cannot be the motive force, nor, all the less so, the leader of the revolution. It is the sworn enemy of the revolution and a stubborn struggle must be waged against it." However, it was precisely in this fundamental question that Stalin was to undergo a complete metamorphosis in the next ten years and was to meet the February revolution of 1917 already as a partisan of a bloc with the liberal bourgeoisie and, in accordance with this, as a champion of uniting with the Mensheviks into one party. Only Lenin on arriving from abroad put an abrupt end to the independent policy of Stalin which he called a mockery of Marxism.

On the Role of the Peasantry

The Narodniks saw in the workers and peasants simply "toilers" and "the exploited" who are all equally interested in socialism. Marxists regarded the peasant as a petty bourgeois who is capable of becoming a socialist only to the extent to which he ceases materially or spiritually to be a peasant. With the sentimentalism peculiar to them, the Narodniks perceived in this sociological characterization a moral slur against the peasantry. Along this line occurred for two generations the main struggle between the revolutionary tendencies of Russia. To understand the future disputes between Stalinism and Trotskyism it is necessary once again to emphasize that, in accordance with the entire tradition of Marxism, Lenin never for a moment regarded the peasantry as a socialist ally of the proletariat. On the contrary, the impossibility of the socialist revolution in Russia was deduced by him precisely from the colossal preponderance of the peasantry. This idea runs through all his articles which touch directly or indirectly upon the agrarian question.

"We support the peasant movement," wrote Lenin in September 1905, "to the extent that it is a revolutionary democratic movement. We are preparing (right now, and immediately) for a struggle with it to the extent that it will come forward as a reactionary, anti-proletarian movement." The entire gist of Marxism lies in this two-fold task. Lenin saw the socialist ally in the Western proletariat and partly in the semi-proletarian elements in the Russian village but never in the peasantry as such. "From the beginning we support to the very end, by means of all measures, up to confiscation," he repeated with the insistence peculiar to him, "the peasant in general against the landlord, and later (and not even later but at the very same time) we support the proletariat against the peasant in general."

"The peasantry will conquer in the bourgeois-democratic revolution," he wrote in March 1906, "and with this it will completely exhaust its revolutionary spirit as the peasantry. The proletariat will conquer in the bourgeois-democratic revolution and with this it will only unfold in a real way its genuine socialist revolutionary spirit." "The movement of the peasantry," he repeated in May of the same year, "is the movement of a different class. This is a struggle not against the foundations of capitalism but for purging all the remnants of feudalism." This viewpoint can be followed in Lenin from one article to the next, year by year, volume by volume. The language and examples vary; the basic thought remains the same. It could not have been otherwise. Had Lenin seen a socialist ally in the peasantry he would not have had the slightest ground for insisting upon the *bourgeois* character of the revolution and for limiting "the dictatorship of the proletariat and the peasantry" to purely democratic tasks. In those cases where Lenin accused the author of this book of "underestimating" the peasantry he had in mind not at all my non-recognition of the socialist tendencies of the peasantry but, on the contrary, my inadequate – from Lenin's viewpoint – recognition of the bourgeois-democratic independence of the peasantry, its ability to create its own power and thereby prevent the establishment of the socialist dictatorship of the proletariat.

The re-evaluation of values on this question was opened up only in the years of Thermidorian reaction the beginning of which coincided approximately with the illness and death of Lenin. Thenceforth the alliance of Russian workers and peasants was proclaimed to be, in and of itself, a sufficient guarantee against the dangers of restoration and an immutable pledge of the realization of socialism within the boundaries of the Soviet Union. Replacing the theory of international revolution by the theory of socialism in one country Stalin began to designate the Marxist evaluation of the peasantry not otherwise than as "Trotskyism" and, moreover, not only in relation to the present but to the entire past.

It is, of course, possible to raise the question whether or not the classic Marxist view of the peasantry has been proven erroneous. This subject would lead us far beyond the limits of the present review. Suffice it to state here that Marxism has never invested its estimation of the peasantry as a non-socialist class with an absolute and static character. Marx himself said that the peasant possesses not only superstitions but the ability to reason. In changing conditions the nature of the peasant himself changes. The regime of the dictatorship of the proletariat opened up very broad possibilities for influencing the peasantry and re-educating it. The limits of these possibilities have not yet been exhausted by history. Nevertheless, it is now already clear that the growing role of the state coercion in the USSR has not refuted but has confirmed fundamentally the attitude toward the peasantry which distinguished Russian Marxists from the Narodniks. However, whatever may be the situation in this respect today after twenty years of the new regime, it remains indubitable that up to the October revolution or more correctly up to 1924 no one in the Marxist Camp – Lenin, least of all – saw in the peasantry a socialist factor of development. Without the aid of the proletarian revolution in the West, Lenin repeated, restoration in Russia was inevitable. He was not mistaken: the Stalinist bureaucracy is nothing else than the first phase of bourgeois restoration.

Trotsky Holds Third Position

We have analyzed above the points of departure of the two basic factions of the Russian Social Democracy. But alongside of them, already at the dawn of the first revolution, was formulated a third position which met with almost no recognition during those years but which we are obliged to set down here with the necessary completeness not only because it found its confirmation in the events of 1917 but especially because seven years after the October revolution, this conception, after being turned topsy-turvy, began to play a completely unforeseen role in the political evolution of Stalin and the whole Soviet bureaucracy.

At the beginning of 1905 a pamphlet by Trotsky was issued in Geneva. This pamphlet analyzed the political situation as it unfolded in the winter of 1904. The author arrived at the conclusion that the independent campaign of petitions and banquets by the liberals had exhausted all its possibilities; that the radical intelligentsia who had pinned their hopes upon the liberals had arrived in a blind alley together with the latter; that the peasant movement was creating favourable conditions for victory but was incapable of assuring it; that a decision could be reached only through the armed uprising of the proletariat; that the next phase on this path would be the general strike. The pamphlet was entitled "Before the Ninth of January," because it was written before the Bloody Sunday in Petersburg. The mighty strike wave which came after this date together with the initial armed clashes which supplemented this strike wave were an unequivocal confirmation of the strategic prognosis of this pamphlet.

The introduction to my work was written by Parvus, a Russian émigré, who had succeeded by that time in becoming a prominent German writer. Parvus was an exceptional creative personality capable of becoming infected with the ideas of others as well as of enriching others by his ideas. He lacked internal equilibrium and sufficient love for work to give the labour movement the contribution worthy of his talents as thinker and writer. On my personal development he exercised undoubted influence especially in regard to the social revolutionary understanding of our epoch. A few years prior to our first meeting Parvus passionately defended the idea of a general strike in Germany; but the country was then passing through a prolonged industrial boom, the Social Democracy had adapted itself to the regime of the Hohenzollerns; the revolutionary propaganda of a foreigner met with nothing except ironical indifference. On becoming acquainted on the second day after the bloody events in Petersburg with my pamphlet, then in manuscript, Parvus was captured by the idea of the exceptional role which the proletariat of backward Russia was destined to play.

Those few days which we spent together in Munich were filled with conversations which clarified a good deal for both of us and which brought us personally closer together. The introduction which Parvus wrote at the time for the pamphlet has entered firmly into the history of the Russian revolution. In a few pages he illuminated those social peculiarities of belated Russia which were, it is true, known previously but from which no one had drawn all the necessary conclusions.

The political radicalism of Western Europe, wrote Parvus, was, as is well known, based primarily on the petty bourgeoisie. These were the handicraft workers and, in general, that section of the bourgeoisie which had been caught up by the industrial development but was at the same time pushed aside by the capitalist class ... In Russia, during the pre-capitalist period, the cities developed more along Chinese than European lines. These were administrative centres, purely functionary in character, without the slightest political significance, while in terms of economic relations they served as trading centres, bazaars, for the surrounding landlord and peasant milieu. Their development was still very insignificant when it was halted by the capitalist process which began to create big cities after its own pattern, i.e., factory cities and centres of world trade ... The very same thing that hindered the development of petty-bourgeois democracy served to benefit the class consciousness of the proletariat in Russia, namely, the weak development of the handicraft form of production. The proletariat was immediately concentrated in the factories.

The peasants will be drawn into the movement in ever larger masses. But they are capable only of increasing the political anarchy in the country and, in this way, of weakening the government; they cannot compose a tightly welded revolutionary army. With the development of the revolution, therefore, an ever greater amount of political work will fall to the share of the proletariat. Along with this, its political self-consciousness will broaden; its political energy will grow.

The Social Democracy will be confronted with the dilemma: either to assume the responsibility for the Provisional Government or to stand aside from the workers' movement. The workers will consider this government as their own regardless of how the Social Democracy conducts itself.... The revolutionary overturn in Russia can be accomplished only by the workers. The revolutionary Provisional Government in Russia will be the government of a *workers' democracy*. If the Social Democracy heads the revolutionary movement of the Russian proletariat, then this government will be Social Democratic.

The Social Democratic Provisional Government will not be able to accomplish a socialist overturn in Russia but the very process of liquidating the autocracy and of establishing the democratic republic will provide it with a rich soil for political work.

In the heat of the revolutionary events in the autumn of 1905, I once again met Parvus, this time in Petersburg. While preserving an organizational independence from both factions, we jointly edited a mass workers' paper, **Russkoye Slovo**, and, in a coalition with the Mensheviks, a big political newspaper, **Nachalo**. The theory of the permanent revolution has usually been linked with the names of "Parvus and Trotsky." This was only partially correct. The period of Parvus' revolutionary apogee belongs to the end of the last century when he marched at the head of the struggle against the so-called "revisionism," i.e., the opportunist distortion of Marx's theory. The failure of the attempts to push the German Social Democracy on the path of more resolute policies undermined his optimism. Toward the perspective of the socialist revolution in the West, Parvus began to react with more and more reservations. He considered at that time that the "Social Democratic Provisional Government will not be able to accomplish a socialist overturn in Russia." His prognoses indicated, therefore, not the transformation of the democratic revolution into the socialist revolution but only the establishment in Russia of a regime of workers' democracy of the Australian type, where on the basis of a farmers' system there arose for the first time a labour government which did not go beyond the framework of a bourgeois regime.

This conclusion was not shared by me. The Australian democracy grew organically from the virgin soil of a new continent and at once assumed a conservative character and subjected to itself a young but quite privileged proletariat. Russian democracy, on the contrary, could arise only as a result of a grandiose revolutionary overturn, the dynamics of which would in no case permit the workers' government to remain within the framework of bourgeois democracy. Our differences, which began shortly after the revolution of 1905, resulted in a complete break between us at the beginning of the war when Parvus, in whom the skeptic had completely killed the revolutionist, turned out on the side of German imperialism, and later became the counsellor and inspirer of the first president of the German republic, Ebert.

The Theory of Permanent Revolution

Beginning with the pamphlet, **Before the Ninth of January**, I returned more than once to the development and justification of the theory of the permanent revolution. In view of the importance which this theory later acquired in the ideological evolution of the hero of this biography, it is necessary to present it here in the form of exact quotations from my works in 1905-06:

The core of the population of a modern city, at least in cities of economic-political significance, is constituted by the sharply differentiated class of wage labour. It is precisely this class, essentially unknown during the Great French Revolution, that is destined to play the decisive role in our revolution ... In a country economically more backward, the proletariat may come to power sooner than in an advanced capitalist country. The assumption of some sort of automatic dependence of proletarian dictatorship upon the technical forces and resources of a country is a prejudice derived from an extremely oversimplified "economic" materialism. Such a view has nothing in common with Marxism ... Notwithstanding that the productive forces of industry in the United States are ten times higher than ours, the political role of the Russian proletariat, its influence upon the polities of the country, and the possibility of its coming influence upon world policies is incomparably higher than the role and significance of the American proletariat.

The Russian revolution, according to our view, will create conditions in which the power may (and with the victory of the revolution *must*) pass into the hands of the proletariat before the politicians of bourgeois liberalism get a chance to develop their statesmanlike genius to the full ... The Russian bourgeoisie is surrendering all the revolutionary positions to the proletariat. It will have to surrender likewise the revolutionary leadership of the peasantry. The proletariat in power will appear to the peasantry as an emancipator class ... The proletariat basing itself on the peasantry will bring all its forces into play to raise the cultural level of the village and develop a political consciousness in the peasantry ... But perhaps the peasantry itself will crowd the proletariat and occupy its place? This is impossible. All the experience of history protests against this assumption. It shows that the peasantry is completely incapable of playing an *independent* political role ... From what has been said it is clear how we regard the idea of the 'dictatorship of the proletariat and the peasantry.' The gist of the matter is not whether we consider it admissible in principle, whether we find this form of political cooperation 'desirable.' We consider it unrealizable-at least in the direct and immediate sense.

The foregoing already demonstrates how erroneous the assertion, later endlessly repeated is, that the conception presented here "leaped over the bourgeois revolution." "The struggle for the democratic renovation of Russia," I wrote at that time, "has wholly grown out of capitalism and is being conducted by the forces unfolding on the basis of capitalism and is being aimed *directly and first of all* against the feudal-serf obstacles on the path of the development of capitalist society." The question, however, was: Just what forces and methods are capable of removing these obstacles?

We may set a bound to all the questions of the revolution by asserting that our revolution is *bourgeois* in its objective aims, and therefore in its inevitable results, find we may thus shut our eyes to the fact that the chief agent of this bourgeois revolution is the proletariat, and the proletariat will be pushed toward power by the whole course of the revolution ... You may lull yourself with the thought that the social conditions of Russia are not yet ripe for a socialist economy – and therewith you may neglect to consider the fact that the proletariat once in power, will inevitably be compelled by the whole logic of its situation to introduce an economy operated by the state ... Entering the government not as impotent hostages but as a ruling power, the representatives of the proletariat will by this very act destroy the boundary between minimum and maximum program, i.e., *place collectivism on the order of the day*. At what point the proletariat will be stopped in this direction will depend on the relationship of forces, but not at all upon the original intentions of the party of the proletariat.

But it is not too early now to pose the question: Must this dictatorship of the proletariat inevitably be shattered against the framework of the bourgeois revolution? Or may it not, upon the given *world-historic foundations*, open before itself the prospect of victory to be achieved by shattering this limited framework? ... One thing can be stated with certainty: Without direct state support from the European proletariat the working class of Russia cannot remain in power and cannot convert its temporary rule into a prolonged socialist dictatorship ..."

From this, however, does not at all flow a pessimistic prognosis:

"The political emancipation led by the working class of Russia raises this leader to unprecedented historical heights, transfers into its hands colossal forces and resources and makes it the initiator of the world liquidation of capitalism, for which history has created all the necessary objective prerequisites."

In regard to the degree to which the international Social Democracy will prove able to fulfil its revolutionary task, I wrote in 1906:

The European socialist parties – above all, the mightiest among them, the German party – have each worked out their own conservatism as an organization embodying the political experience of the proletariat, may become at a certain moment a direct obstacle in the path of the open conflict between the workers and bourgeois reaction ..." I concluded my analysis, however, by expressing assurance that. As greater and greater masses rally to socialism and assurance that the "Eastern revolution will imbue the West proletariat with revolutionary idealism and engender in it the desire to speak to its enemy in 'Russian' ..."

The "Eastern revolutionary idealism and engender in it the desire to speak to its enemy in Russian".

The Three Views Summed Up

Let us sum up. Narodnikism, in the wake of the Slavophiles, proceeded from illusions concerning the absolutely original paths of Russia's development, and waved aside capitalism and the bourgeois republic. Plekhanov's Marxism was concentrated on proving the principled identity of the historical paths of Russia and of the West. The program derived from this ignored the wholly real and not at all mystical peculiarities of Russia's social structure and of her revolutionary development. The Menshevik attitude toward the revolution, stripped of episodic encrustations and individual deviations, is reducible to the following: The victory of the Russian bourgeois revolution is conceivable only under the leadership of the liberal bourgeoisie and must hand over power to the latter. The democratic regime will then permit the Russian proletariat to catch up with its older Western brothers on the road of the struggle for socialism with incomparably greater success than hitherto.

Lenin's perspective may be briefly expressed as follows: The belated Russian bourgeoisie is incapable of leading its own revolution to the end. The complete victory of the revolution through the medium of the "democratic dictatorship of the proletariat and the peasantry" will purge the country of medievalism, invest the development of Russian capitalism with American tempos, strengthen the proletariat in the city and country, and open up broad possibilities for the struggle for socialism. On the other hand, the victory of the Russian revolution will provide a mighty impulse for the socialist revolution in the West, and the latter will not only shield Russia from the dangers of restoration but also permit the Russian proletariat to reach the conquest of power in a comparatively short historical interval.

The perspective of the permanent revolution may be summed up in these words: The complete victory of the democratic revolution in Russia is inconceivable otherwise than in the form of the dictatorship of the proletariat basing itself on the peasantry. The dictatorship of the proletariat, which will inescapably place on the order of the day not only democratic but also socialist tasks, will at the same time provide a mighty impulse to the international socialist revolution. Only, the victory of the proletariat in the West will shield Russia from bourgeois restoration and secure for her the possibility of bringing the socialist construction to its conclusion.

These terse formulations reveal with equal clarity both the homogeneity of the last two conceptions in their irreconcilable contradiction with the liberal-Menshevist perspective as well as their extremely essential difference from one another on the question of the social character and the tasks of the "dictatorship" which was to grow out of the revolution. The frequently repeated objection of the present Moscow theoreticians to the effect that the program of the dictatorship of the proletariat was "premature" in 1905 is entirely lacking in content. In the empirical sense the program of the democratic dictatorship of the proletariat and the peasantry proved to be equally "premature." The unfavourable relation of forces in the epoch of the first revolution rendered impossible not the dictatorship of the proletariat as such but, in general, the victory of the revolution itself. Meanwhile all the revolutionary tendencies proceeded from the hopes for a complete victory; without such a hope an unfettered revolutionary struggle would be impossible. The differences involved the general perspectives of the revolution and the strategy flowing there from. The perspective of Menshevism was false to the core: it pointed out an entirely different road for the proletariat. The perspective of Bolshevism was not complete; it indicated correctly the general direction of the struggle but characterized its stages incorrectly. The inadequacy of the perspective of Bolshevism was not revealed in 1905 only because the revolution itself did not receive further development. But at the beginning of 1917 Lenin was compelled, in a direct struggle against the oldest cadres of the party, to change the perspective.

A political prognosis cannot pretend to the same exactness as an astronomical one. It suffices if it gives a correct indication of the general line of development and helps to orient oneself in the actual course of events in which the basic line is inevitably shifted either to the right or to the left. In this sense it is impossible not to recognize that the conception of the permanent revolution has fully passed the test of history. In the first years of the Soviet regime, this was denied by none; on the contrary, this fact met with recognition in a number of official publications. But when on the quiescent and ossified summits of Soviet society the bureaucratic reaction against October opened up, it was from the very beginning directed against this theory which more completely than any other reflected the first proletarian revolution in history and at the same time clearly revealed its incomplete, limited and partial character. Thus, by way of repulsion, originated the theory of socialism in one country, the basic dogma of Stalinism.

Introduction to "What Is Trotskyism?"

The question that was asked at the beginning of the general introduction could be posed of Ernest Mandel. He was not a founding father of a movement like Marx and Engels, nor did he make a revolution like Lenin and Trotsky. He was, however, a leader and the major theoretician of the Fourth International, the major heir, and upholder of the revolutionary traditions of the other three. Not least of his accomplishments was his work on *Marxist Economic Theory,* a valuable guide to a much defamed subject. He was also an active participant in the revolutionary struggles in Belgium and elsewhere, beginning with his service in the resistance to the Nazi occupation.

Republishing this pamphlet is not just an act of homage to a great Marxist, who would have been first to demand that time and money be spent doing better things if that was the case. There are two other reasons for this work.

The less important of these is that it captures an historic moment when working class revolution was in the air and Mandel and his comrades expected to see their movement lead it, if not to world wide victory, than certainly to decisive victories in a number of countries as a prelude to the international triumph.

This did not happen, of course. There were several reasons for this failure, but the two main ones were the endemic divisions in Trotskyism and the continuing strength of the opposition to it in the workers' movement.

The first was a natural result of the long isolation of the Trotskyist movement before and after the Second World War Splits were always quite frequent in the world socialist movement. Even the Stalinites who prided themselves on their movement's monolithic character depended on the prestige of their base in the world's first workers' state to keep their mainstream united and then found it necessary to expel questioners into the darkness outside. Moreover, when other workers' states were founded, their heads were able to assert alternative authorities and split the movement. Divisions in Trotskyism were inevitable, though it should be said that they were made worse by the practice of what one of the splitters described as 'building Trotsky's party, using Stalin's methods' and resorting to expulsion when honest discussion (as advocated in this work) would have been more fruitful.

The second reason for Trotskyism's failure in this period was the continuing dominance of the workers' movement by social democratic and Stalinite parties. As has been said accurately, 'smallness is not a virtue', and those mass parties attracted more recruits by their very size, appearing to offer more realistic goals than that of Permanent Revolution.

It should be repeated, too, that, as has been said, the implosion of the Soviet Union, due to the problems of maintaining a police state in the name of socialism, and the continuing move rightwards of Social Democracy, that culminated in the betrayals of Blair and Schroder, and will probably not stop with them both had an inevitable negative effect on the environment in which socialism has to be achieved. Nonetheless, as has been remarked in the general introduction, this is unlikely to last and a new generation of aspiring revolutionary socialists will find the heirs of Trotsky far more credible vis-à-vis their rivals. Already, in France, the vote for the old Stalinite Communist Party, once one of the largest in western Europe is smaller than that for the followers of Trotsky, though neither votes compare to that of the Communist Party in its heyday.

In these circumstances, this pamphlet can be a major aid in preparing the new generation for the correct line of struggle. This is the more important reason for republishing it and a reason that is sufficient in itself.

Mandel gives four reasons for his movement's relevance and, despite the changed conditions, they remain valid. The attempts to fight globalisation in the semi-colonial world need to develop permanent revolutionary strategies to be successful. The constitutional road to socialism has failed to maintain momentum in the metropoles and is now being excavated. Above all, the makers of all revolutions have to see their struggle as part of an international one and join together in the fight. On the matter of revolution, the enemy is always essentially at one.

This leaves the need for socialist democracy in the workers' state, and the workers' party. It is well to stress this, since it was its absence that led eventually to the implosion of the USSR and the dash of the peoples of its satellites into globalised capitalism. This lack led to a paralysis of the will to spread the proletarian revolution, lest new *revolutionary* ideas resound in the workers' states themselves. The last soviet leader, Mikhail Gorbachev, found his attempts to revitalise and democratise his state fail because he could not bring himself to expand, or even defend the revolution abroad (his long-term predecessor, Leonid Brezhnev did combine, alongside repression at home, defence of workers' struggles abroad, although he applied it in an often bureaucratic adventurist way, as in Afghanistan). The same failure occurred in the qualitative development of techniques necessary for soviet production to overtake that of capitalism.

For these reasons, Mandel's speech is a valuable guide to socialist revolutionary struggle, and for these reasons it is being reprinted alongside the pieces of Marx Engels, Lenin and Trotsky.

Ernest Mandel: What Is Trotskyism?

The very fact that Monty Johnstone is here debating with me this evening on the problem of Trotskyism today[15] should in itself be considered evidence of what Trotskyism is not. I am not going to insult the intelligence of anyone present by saying that it is not counterrevolutionary or an agency of fascism, or an agency of imperialism, or any of that nonsense. For if that were the case, not only would this debate not take place but many other things which have been happening in the world in the last few years would be incomprehensible.

One thing Trotskyism is not is a defeated tendency in the international workers movement. It is not Menshevik-type revision of Marxism that has been crushed definitively, as was said in the Soviet Union in its fifteenth party congress in 1927; as was repeated by the unfortunate Nikita Sergeivitch Khrushchev at the twentieth party congress of the Communist Party of the Soviet Union in 1956; as has been repeated over and over again in innumerable publications under the control of the Stalinist bureaucracy. Because, if it were really a crushed, defeated, nonexistent, eliminated, Menshevik tendency, why would anybody want to discuss with it? Why is the Soviet bureaucracy after having crushed, destroyed, eliminated and vanquished this tendency, forty, thirty, twenty, and ten years ago, why are the spokesmen for these bureaucrats today forced to write books, pamphlets, and articles and keep coming back to this problem? Why have there been three or four new books on Trotskyism published in the Soviet Union in the last twelve months, if ours is a definitively defeated tendency?

So I think the first point we ought to make this evening is to render historical justice to the founder of the Red Army and to the leader of the insurrection of the October revolution which initiated the first victorious working-class revolution in a whole country. On this ninetieth anniversary of the birth of Leon Trotsky, which coincides with the anniversary of the October revolution, the political movement he founded, the ideas he stood for, the program he defended, live stronger than ever in the world.

There is today a vibrant youth movement. Thousands of young people are coming to Trotskyism all over the world. And that is the only reason Monty Johnstone of the Communist Party feels obliged

---

[15] Speech by Ernest Mandel, delivered in a debate with Monty Johnstone, Editor of the Morning Star, the daily paper of the Communist Party of Great Britain, 7 November 1969.

to debate with us about Trotskyism, that is the only reason why the Soviet bureaucracy has to put out a steady stream of speeches, pamphlets, magazine articles and books on the subject of Trotsky.

Trotskyism today is mainly a youth movement, a movement of youth that is being built and expanded on the five continents. For that very same reason I am not going to dwell in the least on the question that Monty Johnstone is going to talk about quite a lot: What Trotsky wrote or did not write in 1905, in 1912, in 1917, or in 1918. For I want to say from the beginning that this is pretty irrelevant to the actualities of the contemporary revolutionary struggles. Does anyone really think that 250,000 people vote for a Trotskyist presidential candidate in France, does anyone really think that in Ceylon today a Trotskyist trade union leader leads tens of thousands of workers in big strikes, does anyone really think that tens of thousands of people demonstrate behind banners which the whole of public opinion in Japan today calls Trotskyist, because of what Trotsky wrote in 1907 or 1912?

The overwhelming majority of these people have not read what he wrote and are not interested in reading all that – this is a mistake on their part, because everybody should be interested in the history of the revolutionary movement – but they rightly regard that as irrelevant to the main problem which we have to understand and explain: What is the origin, what is the root of the strength of world Trotskyism today, why do thousands and thousands of people flock to its banner on a world scale, and why do the Soviet bureaucrats and Monty Johnstone, their British spokesman, have to reopen a debate which they hoped had been finished with machine-gun bullets thirty or thirty-five years ago, in the period of the infamous Moscow Trials?

I will give four basic reasons why the Trotskyist movement is stronger now than ever before; why thousands of people are adhering to it throughout the world; why it has a bigger numerical, geographical and political extension than ever before, even during the 1920s, while it was still a tendency inside the Communist parties and the Communist International.

The first reason has to do with a basic problem of the colonial revolution and the way forward for the underdeveloped, semicolonial countries. Stalinism and Stalinist parties, parties which call themselves Communist, still follow a Menshevik or semi-Menshevik policy. That is, they believe as the Russian Mensheviks believed, that because these countries are backward, because the industrial bourgeoisie has not yet come to political power, that the immediate strategic task for the working class and poor peasantry is somehow to establish an alliance with this national bourgeoisie against imperialism and against feudal and semi-feudal forces. The aim of such an alliance would be to arrive at a coalition form of government – a "government of the four classes" as it was called in China from 1925 to 1927 – government of the "National Front," or a regime of "National Democracy," as it was called in the new official program of the Soviet Communist Party.

Experience has confirmed what Trotsky's theory of the permanent revolution proclaimed as early as 1906, that there is no way out for any underdeveloped colonial or semicolonial country along such a road; that any struggle that limits itself to fighting against rural feudal or semifeudal landlords, or foreign imperialism, while keeping the national bourgeoisie in power, while maintaining capitalist property relations intact, while refraining from establishing the dictatorship of the proletariat allied to the poor peasantry, will inevitably leave these underdeveloped countries backward, stagnating, exploited and super exploited by international and national capital.

Such a policy will not be able to tear the millions populating these countries out of their age-old miseries. Experience has also taught a much more terrible lesson. Thousands and thousands of Communists in Brazil in 1964, in Iraq in 1958, and five hundred thousand Communists in Indonesia in 1965 had to pay with their lives for the illusion that it was possible, desirable, or necessary to establish durable relationships of coalition and collaboration with bourgeois or semi bourgeois political forces. Such a subordination and sacrifice of independent mass struggle can only lead to a crushing defeat for the working class and the poor peasantry.

Trotskyism lives and grows with new members, attracts new tendencies and builds new parties in the underdeveloped countries because it stands for this basic rule of revolution. There is no way out for these colonial and semicolonial countries but the way of the permanent revolution. There is no possibility of acquiring real national liberation, real independence from imperialism, without overthrowing the bourgeois class together with the agents of foreign imperialism and the feudal and semifeudal landlords. There is no possibility of liberating the people, peasants and workers, without establishing the dictatorship of the proletariat allied with the poor peasantry, without creating a workers state. Only in those countries where this happened – China, Cuba, North Vietnam, and it's happening now in South Vietnam – is there a way to social and economic progress. Wherever, through the responsibility of the Communist parties following the Moscow line, which is Stalinist Menshevism, that has been prevented from happening, there have been defeats, misery, tears and bloodshed for the working people of these countries.

It is this contemporary reality, rather than quotations from 1907, 1917, or 1921, that has to be faced by anyone who wants to understand what is going on in this sector of the world revolution. For the Trotskyist movement, for the revolutionary Marxists throughout the world, it was a moment of great vindication when the leading idea of the permanent revolution – that the only road to victory in a backward country is through a socialist revolution – was taken over by the Cuban revolutionaries and proclaimed in the Second Declaration of Havana, after the first victorious revolution in the Western Hemisphere. This gave proof that Leon Trotsky and the Fourth International had been one hundred per cent correct in their strategic line for the underdeveloped countries.

The second reason for the growth of Trotskyism on a world scale is that we stand completely and unconditionally for the revolutionary road to socialism in the industrialized imperialist countries as against the reformist electoral road defended by the Communist parties in Western Europe, Japan, North America, Australia and New Zealand. When we say that we follow the revolutionary road, this does not mean that we are partisans of putschism or adventurism, that we think a few hundred people here and a few hundred there can snatch power unexpectedly without anybody taking notice of it, in the advanced capitalist countries. There the bourgeoisie represents tremendous power. It has political experience; it has the benefits of political tradition and political continuity. Its rule over these countries does not depend simply and solely upon its weapons of repression – its army and police – but rather upon the ideological and political influence it still wields over a large part of the petty bourgeoisie and even among a part of the working class itself.

Our clear and uncompromising stand in favor of the revolutionary road to socialism essentially pivots around three points:

Firstly, objective situations independent of the will and control of any group or party periodically create prerevolutionary situations in industrially advanced countries. At these moments of revolutionary mass upsurge these objective situations unavoidably lead to large-scale actions of the working class such as general strikes and factory occupations which obviously go beyond the limits of struggle for immediate wage demands and working conditions. The duty of revolutionary parties and groups representing the revolutionary vanguard is to prepare themselves and the best working-class militants to intervene during these hours, days and weeks, for it is only through these periodic upsurges of the mass movement that the chance is presented to overthrow capitalist power.

You cannot overthrow capitalism gradually, you cannot abolish a bourgeois army battalion by battalion, you cannot destroy the power of the bourgeoisie piece by piece. You can only accomplish these aims through the revolutionary mobilization of the masses, and revolutionary actions of this sort are not possible every day when "business as usual" prevails. Revolutionary action is possible only during those prerevolutionary situations when the tension of class relations is at its maximum and the class conflict is sharpest. A party, a vanguard and a class must be prepared to intervene at that juncture in a decisive manner in order to make a breakthrough toward the conquest of power and a victorious socialist revolution.

Secondly, if you want to develop a situation in which the working class wants to know what to do next, in which conditions for revolution are favorable, you must engage in prior propaganda, agitation, and action for transitional demands, especially for the key demand for workers control of production, which crowns all the other demands of the working class in its struggle for power in the industrialized countries. To think that a working class which has been educated, day after day, month after month, year after year, in nothing but immediate trade union demands and electoral politics will in some mysterious way suddenly become capable of revolutionary consciousness and action in a revolutionary situation is to believe in magic or miracles.

Lenin said that the *ABC* of revolutionary policy and the duty of a revolutionary party is to conduct revolutionary propaganda also in periods that are not yet revolutionary. Lenin said that this is precisely what makes the difference between a revolutionary party and a reformist or a centrist party. When revolution does break out, many people suddenly discover their revolutionary soul. But a revolutionary party has the constant duty to propagandize for revolution even if the situation has not yet reached the point of showdown between the classes. Its work in this respect can be an influential factor in accelerating revolutionary consciousness.

Thirdly, we believe that the struggle for transitional demands, for those demands which cannot be incorporated or assimilated into the normal functioning of bourgeois society should not be conducted solely by propagandistic means. Every opportunity should be taken to impel the working class into motion around such demands. They should be introduced into the ongoing daily struggle of the class by all avenues. Unless the workers acquire experience by fighting for these demands in partial struggles they will be unable to generalize their outlook at the height of revolutionary intensity. Otherwise these demands will appear to them as something that falls from the sky, that is imposed from without or advocated only by small minority groups.

I would like to ask Monty Johnstone how he squares the following quotation from Lenin regarding the obligations of a vanguard party with the course followed by the French Communist Party in May 1968. Lenin said:

Will this situation last long; how much more acute will it become? Will it lead to revolution? This is something we do not know, and nobody can know. The answer can be provided only by the *experience* gained during the development of revolutionary sentiment and the transition to revolutionary action by the advanced class, the proletariat. There can be no talk in this connection about "illusions" or their repudiation, since no socialist has ever guaranteed that this war (and not the next one), that today's revolutionary situation (and not tomorrow's) will produce a revolution. What we are discussing is the indisputable and fundamental duty of all socialists – that of revealing to the masses the existence of a revolutionary situation, explaining its scope and depth, arousing the proletariat's revolutionary consciousness and revolutionary determination, helping it to go over to revolutionary action, and forming, for that purpose, organizations suited to the revolutionary situation.

Just compare that quotation, which breathes the spirit of genuine Bolshevism, with the conduct of the Communist parties of France, Italy, Greece, Belgium, and other capitalist countries over the past twenty-five years (not to go still further back to the prewar period), especially with the conduct of the French CP in May 1968, and you will understand both the fundamentally reformist character of these parties and why thousands of young rebels are adhering to Trotskyism in these countries.

The third reason for the growth of Trotskyism today has to do with the crucial question of workers democracy. The main historical goal to be attained in those countries that have already abolished capitalism is the institution of democratically centralized workers self-management in opposition to the material privileges and the monopoly of political and economic power wielded by the bureaucracy. The bureaucratic rulers are the object of hatred by thousands of youth, critically minded intellectuals, and advanced workers in these postcapitalist states. That was graphically evidenced during those few months in the Czechoslovakia of 1968 when these elements of the population had the chance to speak out, at least in part, their real thoughts and feelings.

The bureaucratic regimes in these countries are one of the main reasons for the discrediting of the cause of socialism in the industrialized West which deters much larger numbers of students, intellectuals, and workers from coming out wholeheartedly in favor of a socialist revolution and communism.

What I am referring to is not a full-fledged socialist society, that is to say, a society without any social differentiation, where commodity production and money relations have withered away. Such conditions cannot exist in any of the East European countries today and that is not what is involved in our discussion of their political situation and problems.

What is both possible and urgently called for in the existing situation is what I call a political revolution, a set of changes in the superstructure of the system which would initiate or fulfill the elementary demands of the Marxist and Leninist program on the nature of a dictatorship of the proletariat, leading to the building of a socialist society. In none of the works by Marx or Engels will you find a single sentence, for example, which asserts that the dictatorship of the proletariat means the monopoly of power by a single party.

Nor will you find the slightest support for the abominable notion that the dictatorship of the proletariat means the application of a repressive censorship, not against nonexistent representatives of capitalism and landlordism, but against the working class. These practices have been introduced and implemented by Stalinism.

The invasion of Czechoslovakia by the Kremlin bureaucracy not only violated the sovereignty and independence of a small nation and a fraternal and allied workers state. It was equally criminal in other respects. It identified the suppression of democratic rights such as freedom of expression for workers, students and intellectuals, with the name of communism by taking away from the Czechoslovakian workers the rights they had regained between January and August 1968 to vote independently on resolutions, to have them published in their trade union journals, to criticize the government if they disagreed with its policies and to criticize the managers of their factories.

These were not very extensive rights and they were a far cry from the full-fledged socialist democracy they were entitled to and striving for. Lenin in *State and Revolution* says that under the dictatorship of the proletariat the workers should have a thousand-fold more freedom of self-expression and self-organization than they enjoyed under bourgeois democracy.

Nevertheless, even this elementary right was taken away and hundreds of thousands of soldiers were sent into the Czechoslovak Socialist Republic for that purpose. That was a shameful disgrace. That is why we Trotskyists first have to reestablish what Marxism and Leninism really stand for, because the crimes of Stalinism have so distorted their true content in the minds of many workers.

Socialist democracy involves far more than the self-evident right of the workers to free expression without state censorship or penalties. Socialist democracy means the self-management of the working class on a democratically centralized basis. It means that the workers should run the factories not only as individual and separate units, but the economy as a whole. This requires the subordination of the national planning authorities to the congress of workers councils. It means that the mass of the working class actually exercises the power and determines through its discussions and decisions how the annual national income shall be divided between the consumption and the accumulation funds, that is, between what is used up and enjoyed for immediate needs, and what is set aside and invested for future growth.

Without the possession and exercise of such rights the working class does not really rule, whatever compliments the official propagandists may offer to console it for its lack or loss of power. It is because the Trotskyist program most consistently advocates such democratic rule of the workers that it is bound to win more forces in the Soviet Union and East Europe, where the underlying trends of development are more and more directed toward a political revolution by the masses against the arbitrariness of the bureaucratic autocracy.

Finally, Trotskyism is most noteworthy today for its uncompromising internationalism. After August 1914 and still more after October 1917, Lenin and the Bolsheviks set about to revive the principles and the instrument of internationalism which had been trampled upon by the prewar and pro-imperialist social democratic leaders. One of the most bitter fruits of the anti-Marxist theory of socialism in one country, which Stalin originated and imposed upon world Communism from 1924 on, was the violation and the betrayal of the international solidarity of the working-class struggle. This flouting of internationalism culminated in the scuttling of the Communist International by Stalin in 1943 as a favor to Churchill and Roosevelt.

Now the leaders and followers of international Stalinism are beginning to taste some more of these bitter fruits, which result from subordinating the welfare of the workers movement to the narrow and selfish dictates of the Kremlin bureaucracy. They see the appalling spectacle of the two largest workers states in the world at each other's throats, and even hinting at the possibilities of hostilities between each other. This situation has come about not because either the Soviet or the Chinese masses willed it, but because it is a logical consequence of the despicable petty bourgeois nationalist tendencies and outlooks that guide the bureaucratic strata at the head of these countries today.

The Soviet leaders have gone so far as to encourage and allow so-called communist journalists to talk about "the yellow peril" and to depict the Chinese people as misled by "new Genghis Khans" and as a "menace to civilization." The fact that such utterly reactionary and racist utterances can come from a government and a party that still call themselves communist shows the degree of degeneration to which these organizations have succumbed.

At the height of its power, Stalinism boasted of the monolithic character of the world Communist movement which was bound together by ideological terror and enforced conformity. Now all that is passed. The last Moscow conference of the "World Communist Parties" demonstrated how far disintegration has proceeded. There are hardly two Communist parties which have any measure of autonomy today that think alike and pursue the same line.

They cannot contend against one another and harbor all sorts of divergent tendencies and factions. One can count up to fifteen different "Communist" tendencies on a world scale. The Stalinists used to deride the Trotskyist movement in the past for being ridden by incessant factionalism and splits. They are silent on this score nowadays – and for good reason! None of the splits among the Trotskyists has been comparable to the gigantic fissures that have opened up in the international Communist movement and keep widening from year to year.

Confronted with the tremendous centralized power of the imperialist counterrevolution in the world arena, the youth and the revolutionaries on all continents keenly feel the need for an equivalent centralization of their own forces. They cannot believe that the polycentrism and decentralization that characterize world Stalinism – where the revolutionary movement and the working class in each country is left to its own devices and no one is concerned with the international interests and aims of the struggle for socialism – is ideal. They cannot believe this because it runs counter to the most urgent needs of the struggle of the working masses and to the traditions of Marxism and Leninism.

They were moved to respond so powerfully to Che Guevara's famous appeal for "two, three, many Vietnams" because it corresponded to their innermost urge for an international coordination of their anticolonialist, anti-imperialist, anticapitalist efforts. Che's final message was essentially a call for some central leadership for the world revolution.

This explains why the idea of the Fourth International as a new revolutionary working-class organization carrying on the best traditions of Marxism, which so many dismissed as unreal and utopian, is capturing the minds and stirring the imagination of thousands of young people all over the globe. The socialist revolution cannot advance and certainly cannot triumph on a world scale without the resurgence of the need for a new revolutionary international impressing itself on the consciousness of serious fighters for a new world. The international we want to build and are building will be centralized, but it will not be bureaucratically centralized. It was the bureaucratic centralism of the Stalinist type, that fake centralism which had nothing in common with Lenin's conceptions or organizing the working-class vanguard, which spawned the disintegrated and reactionary tendencies at work in the world Communist movement today. History will prove that democratic centralism, with its freedom of discussion, is not an obstacle but the indispensable vehicle for elaborating a program and implementing united action against the class enemy.

These, then are the four pillars of Trotskyism today: the theory and practice of the permanent revolution, the revolutionary road to socialism through working-class mass action in the advanced capitalist countries, political revolution for socialist democracy in the Soviet bloc and China, and proletarian internationalism. The Fourth International is a growing force on all of the continents because its fundamental ideas express the objective requirements of the world revolutionary process and carry on the ideas of Leninism, of socialism and communism in our epoch.

Notebooks for Study and Research

- 1 The Place of Marxism in History, Ernest Mandel   (40 pp. €5.)
- 2 The Chinese Revolution - I: The Second Chinese Revolution & the Shaping of the Maoist Outlook, Pierre Rousset   (32 pp. €5)
- 3 The Chinese Revolution - II: The Maoist Project Tested in the Struggle for Power, Pierre Rousset   (48 pp. € 5)
- 4 Revolutionary Strategy Today, Daniel Bensaïd   (36 pp. €5)
- 5 Class Struggle and Technological Innovation in Japan since 1945, Muto Ichiyo   (48 pp. €5)
- 6 Populism in Latin America, Adolfo Gilly, Helena Hirata, Carlos M. Vilas, and the Partido Revolucionario de los Trabajadores (Argentina) introduced by Michael Löwy (40 pp. €5)
- 7/8 Market, Plan and Democracy: The Experience of the So-Called Socialist Countries, Catherine Samary   (64pp. €5)
- 9 The Formative Years of the Fourth International (1933-1938), Daniel Bensaïd   (48 pp. €5)
- 10 Marxism & Liberation Theology, Michael Löwy   (40pp € 5)
- 11/12 The Bourgeois Revolutions, Robert Lochhead   (72pp. €5)
- 13 The Spanish Civil War in Euzkadi and Catalonia 1936-39, Miguel Romero   (48pp. €5)
- 14 The Gulf War and the New World Order, André Gunder Frank and Salah Jaber   (72pp. €5)
- 15 From the PCI to the PDS, Livio Maitan   (48pp. €5)
- 16 Do the Workers have a Country?, José Iriarte "Bikila"   (48pp. €5)
- 17/18 October 1917: Coup d'état or Social Revolution, Ernest Mandel   (64pp. €5)
- 19/20 The Fragmentation of Yugoslavia: An Overview, Catherine Samary   (60pp. €5)
- 21 Factory Commitees and Workers' Control in Petrograd in 1917, David Mandel   (48pp. €5)
- 22 Women's Lives in the New Global Economy, Penelope Duggan & Heather Dashner (editors)   (68 pp. € 5)
- 23 Lean Production: Capitalist Utopia? Tony Smith   (68 pp. €5)
- 24/25 World Bank/IMF/WTO: The Free-Market Fiasco, Susan George, Michel Chossudovsky et al.   Out of print
- 26 The Trade-Union Left and the Birth of a New South Africa, Claude Jacquin   (92 pp., €5)

- 27/28 Fatherland or Mother Earth? Essays on the National Question , Michael Löwy (108 pp., €16, £10.99, $16)
- 29/30 Understanding the Nazi Genocide: Marxism after Auschwitz, Enzo Traverso (154 pp., €19.20, £13, $19.)
- 31/32 Globalization: Neoliberal Challenge, Radical Responses, Robert Went (170 pp., €21, £14, $21)
- 33/34 The Clash of Barbarisms: September 11 & the Making of the New World Disorder, Gilbert Achcar (128 pp., €15, £10, $16)
- 35/36 The Porto Alegre Alternative: Direct Democracy in Action, Iain Bruce ed. (162 pp., €19, £13, $23.50)
- 37/38 Take the Power to Change the World, Phil Hearse ed. (144 pp., €9, £6, $12)
- 39/40 Socialists and the Capitalist Recession (with Ernest Mandel's 'Basic Theories of Karl Marx') Raphie De Santos, Michel Husson, Claudio Katz (196 pp., €9, £7, $12)
- 41 Living Internationalism: The IIRE's history, Murray Smith and Joost Kircz eds. (108pp, €5)
- 42/43 Strategies of Resistance & 'Who Are the Trotskyists' Daniel Bensaïd (196 pp. €8, £6, $10)
- 44/45 Building Unity Against Fascism: Classic Marxist Writings, Leon Trotsky, Daniel Guérin, Ted Grant (164 pp., €8, £6, $10)
- 46 October Readings: The development of the concept of Permanent Revolution, D. R. O'Connor Lysaght ed. (110pp, €5)
- 47 The Long March of the Trotskyists: A contribution to the history of the International, Pierre Frank (168 pp €8, £6, $10)
- 48 Women Liberation & Socialist Revolution: Documents of the Fourth International, Penelope Duggan ed. (194pp €8, £6, $10)

Forthcoming

- Marxism and Anarchism, Marx, Lenin, Trotsky et al.
- New Left Parties: Experiences from Europe, Bertil Videt et al.
- Revolution and Counter-revolution in Europe, Pierre Frank
- The conflict in Palestine, Cinzia Nachira ed.
- Dangerous relationships, Marriage and divorces between Marxism and feminism, Cinzia Arruzza
- Returns of Marxism, Sara Farris ed.
- Women and the Crisis, Terry Conway ed.

Subscribe online at: http://bit.ly/NSRsub

To order, email iire@iire.org or write to International Institute for Research and Education, Lombokstraat 40, NL-1094, Amsterdam.